The Achievement of British Pakistani Learners

WORK IN PROGRESS

The report of the RAISE project, 2002-04,
funded by Yorkshire Forward.

compiled by
Robin Richardson and Angela Wood

**The Churches
Regional Commission**
for Yorkshire and the Humber

Trentham Books
Stoke on Trent, UK and Sterling, USA

in association with the Uniting Britain Trust, London

Trentham Books Limited

Westview House	22883 Quicksilver Drive
734 London Road	Sterling
Oakhill	VA 20166-2012
Stoke on Trent	USA
Staffordshire	
England ST4 5NP	

First published 2004

British Library Cataloguing-in-Publication Data
A catalogue record for this book is available from the British Library

1 85856 335 6

Designed and typeset by Trentham Print Design Ltd., Chester and printed in Great Britain by Bemrose Shafron (Printers) Ltd, Chester.

CONTENTS

List of boxes

List of tables

List of figures

BACKGROUND AND ACKNOWLEDGEMENTS

Background

This book arises from a national project in England known as the RAISE project. It was funded by Yorkshire Forward and derived from the work of the Runnymede Trust Commission on British Muslims and Islamophobia in the period 1996-2004. It was organised by the Uniting Britain Trust, in association with the Churches Regional Commission for Yorkshire and the Humber and was coordinated by the Insted consultancy, London.

The project was created because in many parts of England there is a substantial gap between national averages on school attainment and the attainment of pupils of Pakistani and Kashmiri heritage. The project aimed to demonstrate through a series of case studies that the attainment of Pakistani and Kashmiri heritage pupils can be raised and to describe the factors that underlie success.

Participating LEAs

The local authorities involved in the project were Birmingham, Bradford, Calderdale, Derby, Kirklees, Lancashire, Leeds, Leicester, Manchester, Nottingham, Oldham, Redbridge, Rotherham, Sheffield, Slough and Walsall.

Structure of the project

Most of the participating LEAs arranged for one or more case studies to be written about successful practice. All sent a representative to one or more national meetings. These included events in Leeds and also a meeting with officials at the DfES in London.

Website

The project has a website at www.insted.co.uk/raise. The site contains the texts of the case studies on which this book is based and various background information. It will provide information about follow-up.

Schools

Schools which contributed to the project include Allerton Grange School, Leeds; City of Leeds School; Eastborough Junior, Infant and Nursery School, Kirklees; Forest Fields Primary, Nottingham; Kimberworth School, Rotherham; Old Hall School, Rotherham; Primrose High School, Leeds; Quarry Mount Primary, Leeds; Roundhay School, Leeds; and Shakespeare Primary School, Leeds.

Individuals

Individuals who contributed by writing case studies or attending planning meetings, or both, included Anjum Anwar, Shazia Azhar, Davinder Bains, Baljit Billing, Graham Brownlee, Liz Carnelley, Sameena Choudry, Maurice Coles, Jean Clennell, Nicola Davies, Bill Gent, Julie Griffiths-Brown, Judi Hall, Safina Jabeen, Colleen Jackson, Samina Jaffar, Akram Khan-Cheema, Gillian Klein, Rajesh Lall, Gary Lovelace, Musarat Malik, John Martin, Carol McNulty, Joyce Miller, Rehana Minhas, Jo Pilling, Nargis Rashid, Robin Richardson, Kevin Robinson, Tania Sanders, Stuart Scott, Mary Sculthorpe, Jayant Tanna, Talha Wadee, Angela Wood and Liz Wren.

Steering group

The members of the project steering group were Graham Brownlee (Churches Regional Commission for Yorkshire and the Humber), Liz Carnelley (Churches Regional Commission for Yorkshire and the Humber), Akram Khan-Cheema (consultant), Philip Lewis (University of Bradford), Rehana Minhas (Leeds Education), Robin Richardson (Insted), Talha Wadee (Lancashire) and Angela Wood (Insted).

Chapters

Special acknowledgement is due to individuals who provided material for specific chapters: Jannis Abley (chapter 6), Shazia Azhar (chapter 6), Sameena Choudry (chapters 5 and 11), Maurice Irfan Coles (chapters 7 and 11), Nicola Davies (chapters 3 and 4), Monica Deb (chapter 9), Bill Gent (chapter 6), Judi Hall (chapter 11), Colleen Jackson (chapter 11), Samina Jaffar (chapter 6), Musarat Malik (chapter 9), Joyce Miller (chapter 10), Jo Pilling (chapter 6), Tania Sanders (chapter 9), Stuart Scott (chapter 6) and Mary Sculthorpe (chapters 2 and 8).

Statistics

Most of the tabulations, charts and graphs in chapter 3 were created by Nicola Davies. All are from official sources, including in particular the Youth Cohort Study (YCS), the Pupil Level Annual School Census (PLASC) and the Universities and Admissions Advisory Service UCAS).

Responsibility for views expressed

Views expressed or implied in this book are the responsibility of the editors and are not to be understood as necessarily reflecting those of any of the individuals or institutions mentioned above.

Abbreviations and terms

Abbreviations used in this book

A*-C	The top grades in GCSE taken at 16+
BICS	Basic interpersonal communication skills
CALP	Cognitive, academic and linguistic proficiency
DfES	Department for Education and Skills
EAL	English as an additional language
EMA	Ethnic minority achievement
FSM	Free school meals
GCSE	General Certificate of Secondary Education
ICT	Information and communications technology
KS	Key stage
LEA	Local education authority
LFS	Labour force survey
NASUWT	National Association of Schoolmasters and Union of Women Teachers
NCSL	National College of School Leadership
NUT	National Union of Teachers
PLASC	Pupil Level Annual School's Census
QCA	Qualifications and Curriculum Authority
RE	Religious education
RS	Religious studies
SATs	Standard assessment tasks
SEN	Special educational needs
UCAS	Universities
YCS	Youth cohort study

Terms

'Pakistani'

The vast majority of people in Britain referred to as 'Pakistani' in censuses and surveys, and in everyday conversations, are British citizens of long standing. The word 'Pakistani' on its own, therefore, is misleading and harmful insofar as it implies non-British. Compound terms such as 'Pakistani-British' and Pakistani heritage' (as for example in the phrase 'Pakistani heritage pupils in schools') are frequently preferable.

'Kashmiri'

Many people of Pakistani heritage in Britain define themselves as Kashmiris. This self-definition is taken into account in surveys conducted by certain local authorities but not in national surveys and statistics. From time to time in this book the phrase 'Pakistani and Kashmiri heritage' is used in order to reflect and respect usage in the communities themselves, and to signal that there are significant differences within the large group referred to in national statistics with the single term 'Pakistani'.

'Muslim'

When the national census of population asked about people's religion in 2001 the concern was with affiliation and background, not about personal beliefs or about involvement in religious activities and practices. The term 'Muslim', for example, referred to heritage and sense of belonging and not necessarily to the beliefs which people may or may not hold, or to practices in which they may or may not engage. In this book, similarly, the term 'Muslim' refers primarily to affiliation and heritage.

Transliterations

This book uses the following transliterations of Arabic terms: *hafiz* (scholar who has memorised the Qur'an), *madrasah* (place of teaching and learning) and *Qur'an*.

The RAISE project

The deputy head of a secondary school undertook, on behalf of the school's senior management team, to consider what could and should be done at the school to raise the achievement of Pakistani heritage students. An obvious starting point was to ask a cross-section of students themselves what they thought the key issues were. So she arranged for a small focus group discussion in her room. However, she did not tell the students in advance what precisely the purpose and subject-matter of the meeting would be – she thought the meeting would get off to a bad start if she were to come straight out and say directly what her concerns were. An indirect, softly-softly approach, she thought, would be best.

In thinking this, she was reflecting the views of many of her colleagues. They were reluctant to focus on the achievement of any one group of students, particularly *this* group in the current climate of public opinion.

As the group of students was still assembling the deputy had to leave the room for a few moments. As she returned she overheard a scrap of conversation. 'Does anyone know why we've all been called together?' asked one of the students. 'Well,' said another, 'from looking round at who's here, I should think it's something to do with Pakistani under-achievement.'

The meeting took place in 2003 within the framework of a national project known as the RAISE project, funded by the Yorkshire Forward regional development agency. The project's purpose was to report on work in progress in local authorities and schools throughout the country to reduce and remove inequalities between the achievement of Pakistani and Kashmiri heritage young people and national averages, and to offer reflections and tentative conclusions. This book is the outcome.

The project involved raising and discussing a range of sensitive and controversial issues, as the deputy head mentioned above was all too aware. But one of its

foundations was the belief that hard issues need to be dealt with explicitly and openly, rather in the style of the students quoted above, who were so much more relaxed and forthright than their teachers.

Twenty local authorities were approached and invited to send representatives to a preliminary meeting in Leeds. In due course eleven authorities wrote case studies about work in which they were involved. These papers have been extensively used and quoted for the compilation of this composite report.

The report begins with three introductory chapters, respectively about historical background, pressures on young people and statistics about achievement.

The following seven chapters are based on stories and enquiries in local settings. There is a report on debates, discussions and disagreements in Slough (chapter 4); a survey of student opinions, reflections and outlook in Sheffield (chapter 5); an account of work with parents in Kirklees, Nottingham and Redbridge (chapter 6); discussion of contacts and cooperation between schools and mosques in Leicester and Redbridge (chapter 7); a description of inservice training at a new school in Rotherham (chapter 8); reviews from Derby and Kirklees of ways to help develop academic English (chapter 9); and a report on citizenship education in Bradford (chapter 10). The final chapter (11) is about school leadership and draws on work in schools in Leeds and Sheffield.

There is a fuller, chapter-by-chapter summary later in this introduction.

At one of the national planning meetings, participants discussed ways of visualising the themes of the project as a whole. They came up with the idea of a triangle. In the middle of the triangle is the individual child – a particularly important emphasis since many of the RAISE case studies involved listening and attending to children and young people. The three corners of the triangle are the school, the home and the mosque. Amongst the streams and crosscurrents that flow

between these three points, British Pakistani children and teenagers navigate their way.

Home

CHILD

School · Mosque

The key words at the corners do not refer to simple entities. There is huge diversity within and between schools and in homes and mosques. Each area is amorphous and complex and is not accurately represented by a single point. Each has attractions but also each contains pressures that young people, as they seek their own way in life, may wish to resist. The triangle exists within a wider context of social and economic change and of political debates and controversy, locally, nationally and globally,

This report, accordingly, is about work in progress, not about final products. It's a scrapbook not a showcase, a set of jottings and cuttings from a journey, not the portrait of a destination.

Thanks and acknowledgements are due to all who gave the RAISE project financial, moral and organisational support. They include Yorkshire Forward, the Churches' Regional Commission for Yorkshire and the Humber and the Uniting Britain Trust. Thanks are due also to all the people who participated in the project, directly as writers and compilers of case studies or indirectly by being interviewed or answering questionnaires. Some of the teachers in the project, like the deputy head and her colleagues mentioned above, had to cope with uncertainties and complexities for which they felt unprepared – so thanks also to the pupils and students who came to their rescue.

And good wishes are due to all readers who find in these pages a reflection of their own concerns and situations, and of their own work in progress.

CHAPTER-BY-CHAPTER SUMMARY

Chapter 1
'What I think of myself' – identities, communities and history

Chapter 1 begins by quoting from a conversation amongst four 14-year-old school students. The conversation is about how they see themselves and about the principal components of their identities, 'Asian', 'British', 'Muslim' and 'Pakistani'. The chapter then recalls the historical background – how and why the grandparents of these four students came to Britain in the 1950s and 1960s, and the principal events and trends affecting the Pakistani community in Britain in the 70s, 80s and 90s. It stresses that Pakistani British people are 'a community of communities', not a monolithic bloc, and that particular attention needs to be paid in the education system to those whose origins are in Azad Kashmir, and for whom being Kashmiri is an important part of their identity.

Chapter 2
'If he doesn't look deeply at himself' – pressures and choices for the young

Young British Pakistanis and Kashmiris, like all other young British people, seek and shape their identities within a range of influences and pressures. Some of the influences are mutually compatible and they therefore reinforce each other. Others, however, conflict with each other and in consequence young people are pulled in opposite directions. There are recollections in this chapter about family life; the mosque and mosque-based education; new developments in Islamic theology and spirituality; street culture and youth culture; and currents of thought and influence loosely known as 'fundamentalism' or 'political Islam'.

Chapter 3
Life chances – achievement and progress in the education system

All schools declare that their aim is to raise academic standards. With regard to the standards achieved by Pakistani and Kashmiri heritage learners in English schools, there are four principal sources of statistical information: the Youth Cohort Study (YCS), the Pupil Annual School Census (PLASC), the Universities and Admissions Advisory Service UCAS), and monitoring and committee reports produced in individual local education authorities (LEAs). Information about participation in employment training and adult education is collected and published through the Labour Force Survey (LFS). All these

sources of statistics show that Pakistani heritage learners are achieving below national averages. At the same time, other statistics show that Pakistani heritage families and households are disproportionately affected by poverty and social exclusion. For example, nearly 40 per cent of all Pakistani heritage learners in secondary schools are affected by poverty, as measured by eligibility for free school meals, compared with a national average of fewer than 20 per cent. Chapter 3 reviews the evidence and the implications.

Chapter 4
What's going on? – interpreting and debating data

Chapter 4 continues the focus in the previous chapter on statistics. It describes how statistics about achievement in one particular local authority were analysed and interpreted. The authority in question generally has higher standards amongst its Pakistani heritage learners than many other authorities and the chapter discusses why this might be so. But recently the GCSE results for such learners were disappointingly poor. The chapter considers why this may have happened and quotes the views of Pakistani heritage professionals. A recurring emphasis amongst them was that Islamophobia has a significant impact on both teachers and learners. The chapter is based on a paper by Nicola Davies, an educational consultant who was until recently a teacher in Slough.

Chapter 5
Magic ingredients? – the views and reflections of young people

Chapter 5 is similar to the previous chapter in that it is based on analysis of statistics and on enquiries with people deeply immersed in the realities to which the statistics refer. In this instance the people who were consulted were students in two secondary schools. Statistics had enabled a local authority to identify secondary schools which were bucking the trend in relation to the achievement of Pakistani heritage learners. A researcher met with some of the high-achieving students themselves and obtained their own angle on the factors underlying their success. The chapter is based on a paper by Sameena Choudry, currently head of the Lincolnshire bilingual support service and until recently a teacher adviser in Sheffield.

Chapter 6
Not just writing letters – consulting and working with parents

There is substantial research evidence that the achievement of children and young people in school is related to the kinds of relationship that schools build and maintain with parents. Chapter 6 is based on work with parents in Kirklees, Nottingham and Redbridge and refers also to a publication developed in Oldham. It draws on reports by Jo Pilling and Shazia Azhar, who are members of the EMA service in Kirklees; Stuart Scott, working as a consultant in Nottingham; and Jannis Abley and Samina Jaffar, members of the EMA service in Redbridge.

Chapter 7
Being a British Muslim – linking with mosques, imams and madrasahs

Working closely with parents is essential, as outlined in the previous chapter. Chapter 7 discusses the essential importance of working in partnership with mosques and madrasahs, and of understanding Islamic concepts of education, knowledge and learning. In this context it describes a partnership between a cluster of schools in Leicester and four madrasahs and refers also to a mentoring scheme in Redbridge involving two local imams. It closes with advice to mainstream schools, LEAs and the complementary sector. It is based primarily on a paper by Maurice Irfan Coles, chief executive of the School Development Support Agency and previously a senior adviser in Birmingham.

Chapter 8
They can't just stand there – preparing and training staff

Are there specific skills, strategies, insights and understandings that teachers need to have and to use in schools which have substantial numbers of Pakistani heritage learners? If so, what are they? And how are they developed? These questions are particularly apposite and urgent when a school's student population changes quite suddenly, for example as a result of merging with another school. Chapter 8 describes how a secondary school in Rotherham set about preparing for a major change in its student population. It is based on a paper by Mary Sculthorpe, who is the EMA coordinator at Kimberworth School, Rotherham. At the time that the paper was written, Kimberworth was in the process of merging with Old Hall School.

Chapter 9
Cat have two mouses – moving to academic English

For most British children of Pakistani and Kashmiri heritage, English is an additional language. When they start nursery or infant school they fairly quickly develop basic interpersonal communication skills in English, and soon appear to speak English as fluently as do children for whom English is the mother tongue. However, they do not as readily develop the kinds of formal, abstract language that is required, both orally and writing, for academic progress. Various kinds of focused intervention, therefore, are required. Chapter 9 describes two action research projects concerned with fostering academic English. The first took place in an inner-city infant school in Derby and used a programme first developed in Bradford. The second took place in the mathematics and science departments of some schools in Kirlees. The chapter draws on papers by Tania Sanders, who is an advisory teacher in Derby, and Monica Deb, a member of the EMA service in Kirklees.

Chapter 10
Many views, one landscape – developing the citizenship curriculum

What principles should underlie the citizenship curriculum, and what should be the core objectives and programmes of study, the content, the methodology? In what ways and under what circumstances may the citizenship curriculum lead to higher achievement for Pakistani heritage learners? These are the questions discussed in chapter 10. The chapter describes how an enhanced citizenship curriculum is being developed in Bradford. It is based largely on a report by Joyce Miller, who is a member of Education Bradford's inspection and advisory service.

Chapter 11
Doing something right

If the tasks outlined in previous chapters are to be successfully implemented, the role of headteachers and other senior staff is clearly pivotal. Chapter 11 draws on interviews with senior staff in Sheffield; describes developments in schools in Leeds identified by the local authority as successful in raising the achievement of Pakistani heritage learners; and draws together threads and themes from all the previous chapters. and proposes principles to guide further policy and action.

1 WHAT I THINK OF MYSELF
Identities, communities and history

SUMMARY
This chapter begins by quoting from a conversation amongst four 14-year-old school students about how they see themselves It then recalls the historical background – how and why the grandparents of these four students came to Britain in the 1950s and 1960s from West Pakistan. It stresses that Pakistani British people are 'a community of communities', not a monolithic bloc, and that particular attention needs to be paid in the education system to Kashmiri communities.

'Do you like being called British Asian?' Shakeel asks a group of friends. 'I like Paki better. I'm a Paki. What do you think?' Kiran replies: 'I think of myself as a British Asian Muslim.' Samina says: 'I'm a Muslim, I believe in Islam.' And Shazad: 'I don't think of myself as a Muslim and I don't think of myself as a Pakistani... I *may* be a Muslim, but I don't think of myself as Muslim. I think of myself as a British Asian, that is what I think of myself.'[1]

Shakeel, Kiran, Samina and Shazad were all aged 14 when they had that particular conversation in summer 2003. The answers they gave to themselves and each other that day showed a lively interest in their own being and becoming – their own personal, cultural and national identity. The answers showed also that they are continually pondering, probing, choosing, developing.

This book is about people such as Shakeel, Kiran, Samina and Shazad, and about their brothers and sisters; about the futures they are creating for themselves in modern Britain; about their parents and community and their local mosque and madrasahs; about conflicting pressures on them and how they balance and make sense of these; and, especially, about their experiences and aspirations in the school system. The book is intended in particular for teachers in mainstream schools. Parts of it, though, are likely to be of interest and use also to teachers in madrasahs. And parts, it's reasonable to hope, will intrigue Shakeel, Kiran, Samina and Shazad themselves.

This opening chapter contains a brief sketch of history, to recall where these young people are coming from. The following chapter outlines the pressures on them, to recall the range of futures and places they may be going to. The third chapter is about how they are getting on at school. The rest of the book is about practical implications for their teachers.

The early pioneers
The grandfathers of Shakeel, Kiran, Samina and Shazad, it may be imagined, came to Britain in the early 1950s as young men looking for work. They had grown up in the Mirpur district of Azad Kashmir in what is now Pakistan.[2] There is a longstanding tradition there of young men leaving home for a few years to earn money for their family. These particular young men chose Britain because they or their friends and relatives had served in the British army or in the British merchant navy during the second world war. Also, their energy, determination and readiness for hard work were desperately needed by the British economy – there were tasks of post-war reconstruction to be seen to, and new manufacturing processes meant there was a great demand for people to work night shifts in Britain's textiles and steel industries.

The young Pakistanis who came in the 1950s took on jobs and working conditions that the indigenous British refused to accept for the wages on offer. They lived together in all-male households and concentrated on earning and saving money to send home. From time to

time they went back to Pakistan (West Pakistan, as it was in those days) for extended periods and whilst there they got married and started families. They took for granted that one day they would go back for good. There was no need for them to learn more than basic English, and in any case they encountered great hostility and racism from English people they encountered. They were not invited by the English to integrate into English society.

Around 1960-62, the young husbands were faced with a choice. They either had to return to their families in West Pakistan or else they had to bring their families to Britain. Large numbers, including the grandfathers of Shakeel, Kiran, Samina and Shazad, chose the latter option. In consequence they began to see themselves as settlers, not as migrant workers – though 'the myth of return', as academics call it, persisted for at least two more decades. Certainly the children of the pioneer generation saw themselves as British, however, particularly those who were born here in the course of the 60s and 70s. And so did their grandchildren, born in the 1990s.

Of the eight parents of Shakeel, Kiran, Samina and Shazad, it may be imagined that four were born in Britain, two came to Britain as small children and two came in young adulthood as brides or bridegrooms. When talking with their grandparents and mothers, Shakeel, Kiran, Samina and Shazad converse in the language they learnt first when they were toddlers, variously known as Punjabi, Pahari or Mirpuri. They use English when talking with each other and with their brothers and sisters. Also, more often than not, they speak English with their fathers. They readily understand the spoken language known as Urdu/Hindi that is used in movies and videos and are beginning to study written Urdu as a modern foreign language at GCSE. From their attendance at madrasahs, they can read, write and recite Qur'anic Arabic. The terms 'bilingual' and 'EAL' to describe them are therefore misleading and do not do justice to their substantial linguistic agility and prowess.

Box 1

Look first at industrial history – the roots of the present

... We have to look first at the industrial history of the town. In the late 19th century, Oldham produced 30 per cent of the world's spun cotton, and a very large proportion of the machinery used in textile production. Other industries had a foothold in Oldham, and at one time there was significant coal-mining, but their importance compared with cotton spinning was always minor, and there were few towns as wholly dependent on one industry as Oldham.

This had two main consequences relevant to our review. The first was that much of the employment in Oldham was relatively low skilled and, except for a few boom periods, relatively low paid. Despite efforts to improve the employment base of the town as the cotton industry declined Oldham has remained, relatively, a poor town.

... The second consequence of heavy dependence on a single industry was that, as working conditions and expectations improved in the nation generally it became harder for mill owners to recruit people for unsocial work such as night shifts which were essential to the economy of their enterprises. So people willing to work these shifts were encouraged to migrate, initially from Pakistan, later from Bangladesh, which laid the foundations for the current Pakistani and Bangladeshi communities within the town. The first group of these migrants began to arrive in the 1960s, men first, followed by their families.

The early arrivals from Pakistan formed a community which was culturally very distinct from the white population, in dress, in language, in religion and other customs, as well of course as colour. The majority came from the same area, Mirpur, and working the night shift as a group meant that they had less contact with white society, and the English language, than many immigrants. While other groups of immigrants had shared some of their differences from the indigenous population, none had shared all of them, and the degree of difference undoubtedly made the challenge of achieving an acceptable level of integration harder. It has not yet been achieved, and the progress over the last 40 years has been unacceptably low.

Source: One Oldham One Future (the Ritchie report), 2001

History in one town

The life-stories of the families of Shakeel, Kiran, Samina and Shazad can be filled out with reference to just one of the towns where people from Pakistan settled. In 2001, a report on Oldham included a brief history of the town as a prelude to discussing its present challenges and future development. There are broad similarities between Oldham and several other towns or cities in England where Pakistani heritage people are settled, and it is relevant therefore to quote from the report. Box 1 refers to trends and concerns that are widespread, not limited to Oldham alone.

In the early1970s one of the school pupils in Oldham was Lee Jasper, who two decades later would be an adviser on race equality issues to the Mayor of London. Immediately after the disturbances that rocked the town and the whole nation in summer 2001, he wrote an article in which he recalled his teenage years. He described teachers in the 1970s as 'unreconstructed racists', no different in their attitudes from the foul-mouthed police officers whom he and his friends encountered on the streets. He said that they regarded having to teach black and Asian pupils as 'an insult both to their professional standing and to their notion of Empire'. There is a fuller extract from his article in Box 2.

Many other black and Asian people who were at school in Britain in the 1970s have memories and perspectives similar to those of Lee Jasper. Such memories are corroborated by white people who were teachers or LEA officers in the 1970s. One such person recalls a secondary headteacher who openly declared in 1979 that his job, in relation to the South Asian pupils at his school, was 'to get rid of their strange and funny ways – their gibberish language, their silly clothes, their awful food, their strange and funny religion.'

Lee Jasper and his contemporaries are now the parents of the generation to which Shakeel, Kiran, Samina and Shazad belong. They would probably acknowledge that teachers nowadays are rather different from the ones that they had to deal with when they were young. They suspect, however, that there are still low expectations and negative stereotypes in at least some staffroom cultures, and that this is one of the reasons their children do not have the success at school that they want for them. Meeting failure at school, the children turn for moral support and personal dignity to each other and to street culture. In Lee Jasper's words they are all too ready then, when provoked, to 'react like a cornered tiger'. There is further discussion of the attractions and nature of street culture in the next chapter.

Patterns and history of settlement

The imagined family history of Shakeel, Kiran, Samina and Shazad, and the real history of Oldham and the real reminiscences of Lee Jasper and his contemporaries, can readily be placed within the wider

---

Box 2

The attitudes of the time
– distaste and extreme prejudice

Unemployment in the 70s brought the town to its knees. At that time we young black people were in the process of breaking the hearts of our parents by rebelling against a school system that found it impossible to deal with us... Education was typical of the attitudes of the time: the posh kids got all the attention ... The teachers were in the main ex-grammar-school, unreconstructed racists. That they were forced to teach blacks and Asian children was an insult both to their professional standing and to their notion of Empire. They made their distaste known by the expression of their extreme prejudice. They simply refused to teach us.

'Police racism was cruel, violent and unremitting. Once my mother was trying to find out why I was in a police car. She was told by the officer: 'Fuck off, you nigger bitch.' Police response to victims of racial attacks was: 'If you don't like it, move.'

'...It ought to be no surprise that communities suffering such extreme economic marginalisation and social segregation should seek to defend themselves. There is a historical failure of the town to challenge its own institutional racism. Islands of exclusion imprison within them boundless talent and creativity, confined by sheer walls of discrimination and lack of opportunity. People will inevitably cleave tightly to the central tenets of their culture and faith. Occasionally when provoked they will react like a cornered tiger.

Source: Lee Jasper, Brickbats for Oldham, *The Guardian*, 29 May 2001

---

national context. People from the country now called Pakistan have lived in Britain since the nineteenth century. But it was in the 1950s that migration began on a large scale. Migration mainly involved men in the first instance. In Bradford in 1961, for example, all but 81 of the 3,376 Pakistanis in the city were men. Migration was encouraged because there were major labour shortages in Britain, particularly in the steel and textiles industries of Yorkshire, Lancashire and the West Midlands, and particularly for night shifts. In southern England the main places of Pakistani settlement were Luton and Slough, where the principal sources of employment were in light industry.

The workers who came were needed by the economy. They were actually or in effect invited by employers. As Commonwealth citizens they had full rights of entry and residence, and full civic rights. They came principally from Punjab Province in West Pakistan (now known as Pakistan), from the north western part of Kashmir administered by Pakistan, known as Azad Kashmir, or from the Sylhet area of the country now known as Bangladesh, but then as East Pakistan.

In all of these largely rural areas there was a longstanding tradition of young men migrating for lengthy periods to other countries or regions to raise money for their families back home. The migration to Britain was thus from a rural setting to an urban one as well as to a different country and culture, and involved an increase in wealth and income as well as a change of occupation. In the case of the Mirpuris it was affected by the building of the Mangla Dam on the river Jhelum in the years following independence. The dam displaced the populations of some 250 villages, about 100,000 people altogether. Many of the villagers received compensation money and some used a portion of this to finance their journey to Britain.

In addition to those who came from rural areas, significant numbers of Pakistani settlers in the 1960s were from towns and cities. A high proportion of these had professional qualifications in teaching, medicine or engineering. Many of them had their family roots in post-1947 India rather than in Pakistan itself. They tended to settle in London rather than in the Midlands or North.

The Pakistani community in Britain is thus a community of communities, not a monolithic whole.

There are substantial differences in terms of the areas of Pakistan from which people originated and their original socio-economic position before they migrated; the pattern of push-and-pull factors which affected their original migration; the areas of the British economy which they joined when they first arrived and the economic history of those areas since the 1960s; and their current employment status, social class and geographic location. At an inquiry in Bradford in the 1990s a witness gave a vivid account of the complexity of identity and community from his own point of view. All Pakistani British people experience broadly similar complexities and richness:

> I could view myself as a member of the following communities, depending on the context and in no particular order: Black, Asian, Azad Kashmiri, Mirpuri, Jat, Marilail, Kungriwalay, Pakistani, English, British, Yorkshireman, Bradfordian, from Bradford Moor ... I could use the term 'community' in any of these contexts and it would have meaning. Any attempt to define me only as one of these would be meaningless.

In the Midlands and the North, and also in towns such as Luton and Slough, the vast majority of Pakistanis (probably 85 per cent or more) have their roots in Azad Kashmir. Much more than is the case with Pakistanis in London (who in any case largely have their origins in other parts of Pakistan) they have been severely affected by changes in the British economy, particularly steel and textiles industries, since the 1970s. The collapse of the industries they originally came to work in has meant that many of them are now living in considerable poverty. Compared with the rest of the population, British Pakistani children are more likely to be living in workless households and in households where there is serious ill health. At least two fifths of them are eligible for free school meals, compared with a national average of less than one fifth. The problems of poverty are exacerbated by racism on the streets (British Pakistani and Bangladeshi people are far more likely to be targeted in racist attacks and abuse than any other community) and by pervasive anti-Muslim hostility in the media.

Developing as Muslims

In the early days, most Pakistani migrants to Britain saw themselves as temporary visitors who would one day return to their country of origin, but a turning point came in 1961. It was then that the UK government began to restrict migrant workers through the Commonwealth Immigration Act. There was an eighteen month gap between the passing of the Act and its enforcement and this provided time for the young Pakistani men to take stock. Did they really want to return to their country of origin, as they had always hitherto expected and planned? Or did they want to make Britain their home?

For a range of reasons, the vast majority chose to settle. By 1964, the Ministry of Labour had stopped granting permission for the unskilled to work in Britain. One impact of this legislation was that men who had formerly shared a house with others now began looking for houses for their families. A second was that with the arrival of wives and children there was a desire to impart religious education by teaching the basic beliefs and the practices of Islam. This meant allocating a house for their children's education in the neighbourhood and using the same house for the five daily prayers. Islamic dietary laws saw the development of halal butcher shops. Imams were brought from Azad Kashmir to lead worship. Although more consciously Muslim than previously in their sense of identity, and more observant in the practice of their faith, the settlers did not readily distinguish between components of Islam that are universal and components that are distinctive of rural Kashmir. This was by no means surprising, but it did contribute to later problems.

Before 1964 only seven new mosques had been registered in Britain. But in 1964 itself a further seven were registered and over the next decade there were about eight new registrations each year. From 1974 onwards new registrations were running at 25-30 a year.[3] The creation of mosques was both a cause and a consequence of increased Islamic observance and Muslim self-definition. In the first instance most mosques were converted from existing buildings. But increasingly from the 1970s onwards they were purpose-built. In autumn 1996 it was estimated that there were 613 mosques in Britain, of which 96 were purpose-built.

Researchers at the Policy Studies Institute in the mid 1990s asked a wide range of British people about the importance of religion in their lives. About three quarters of the Muslim respondents said that religion was very important and four in five Muslim men over the age of 35 reported that they visit a mosque at least once every week.

This strengthening of religious belief and practice was influenced by:

☐ the desire to build a sense of corporate identity and strength in a situation of material disadvantage, and in an alien and largely hostile surrounding culture

☐ the need, now that communities contained both children and elders, to keep the generations together

☐ wishing to transmit the community's values to children and young people

☐ the search for inner spiritual resources to withstand the pressures of racism and Islamophobia, and the threat to South Asian culture and customs posed by western materialism and permissiveness.

There were other influences as well. The increased influence of Islam in the politics of Pakistan in the 1970s was a significant factor, as was the increased influence in international affairs of oil-exporting countries, most of which were Muslim. Both of these trends contributed to Muslim self-confidence and assertiveness within Britain. In addition, and even more importantly, a sense of community strength grew through the 1980s out of successful local campaigns to assert Muslim values and concerns, for example for halal food to be served in schools and hospitals, and from the extremely high-profile campaign to protest against the insulting vilification of Islam, as Muslims in Britain almost unanimously saw it, perpetrated by Salman Rushdie's *The Satanic Verses*.

More recently, there has been successful advocacy nationally for the recognition of Muslim identities in public life. Notable developments include changes in employment law, so that Muslims are now protected from direct and indirect discrimination in employment; changes in the criminal justice system, so that crimes against Muslims may attract higher sentences if they are deemed to be aggravated by anti-Muslim hostility;

the appointment of Muslims to take chaplaincy roles in hospitals, prisons and universities; changes in the financial services industry to accommodate Muslim beliefs and values relating to loans; a new sensitivity to the dangers of Islamophobia in the media; and a wide range of organisations and websites devoted to the interests and needs of British Muslims. Whether these advances prove to be real and lasting or whether there will be retreat from them remains to be seen.[4]

Islamophobia and 'fundamentalism'

Problems of coping with secularism, and distinguishing between Islam in general and Punjabi/Mirpuri traditions and culture in particular, were exacerbated by rising levels of Islamophobia – alternatively known as anti-Muslim racism – throughout the 1990s. There is further discussion of Islamophobia in the next chapter.

Simultaneously there was a growth world-wide in so-called fundamentalism or political Islam and this was readily attractive to some Pakistani British young men in their late teens and early 20s. In summer 2001 there were disturbances in northern cities involving young Pakistani British males and these had a profound effect throughout the country. Some of the issues raised by them were well summarised in an article in *The Times* by Raymond Whitaker. There is an extract from his article in box 9 in the next chapter.

Concluding note

This chapter has outlined the historical, cultural and social context in which Shakeel, Kiran, Samina and Shazad are building their identities and futures and in which they engage with the education system. The same context affects their teachers, both in madrasahs and in mainstream schools. The next chapter discusses in greater detail the range of pressures and influences bearing upon them.

First, before this introductory chapter ends, there are some statistics about British Pakistani pupils in the English school system. How many are there and whereabouts in England do they mostly live? Table 1 gives the answers. It is derived from figures published by the DfES following its survey of the school population in January 2003.

Table 1 shows that in January 2003 there were 175,100 pupils of Pakistani heritage in English primary and secondary schools. Rather more than half (98,810, or 56 per cent) were in primary schools. Nearly a half (45.5 per cent) were in just two regions, the West Midlands and Yorkshire and Humber. The other two regions with substantial numbers were London (17.5 per cent) and the North West (16.8 per cent). Further, there are pupils of dual heritage, with one parent of Pakistani heritage. It is not known how many of the 93,290 pupils of mixed Asian and white heritage or 'any other mixed background' have a Pakistani parent.

In addition to the 169,080 pupils in primary and secondary schools, there were 2,902 Pakistani heritage

Table 1: Pupils of Pakistani heritage in English schools, 2003

Region	Primary schools	Secondary schools	Total	Percentage
North East	1,680	1,270	2,950	1.7
North West	17,140	12,320	29,460	16.8
Yorkshire and Humber	22,260	17,380	39,640	22.6
East Midlands	4,040	2,730	6,770	3.9
West Midlands	23,200	16,960	40,160	22.9
East of England	5,430	4,380	9,810	5.6
London	16,630	14,000	30,630	17.5
South East	7,740	6,730	14,470	8.3
South West	690	520	1,210	0.7
Totals	**98,810**	**76,290**	**175,100**	**100.0**

Source- Statistics of Education: Schools in England 2003 Edition

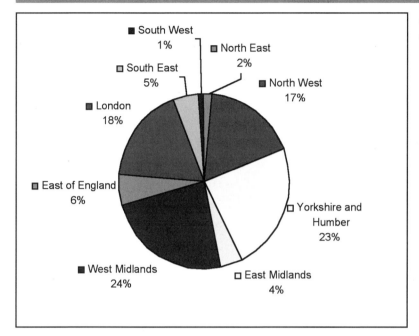

Figure 1: Pakistani heritage pupils by region, 2003

pupils in special schools. The total in all three sectors was therefore 178,002.

The age-profile of Pakistani communities in Britain is different from that of the population as a whole. A higher proportion of Pakistani heritage people are under twenty, and a lower proportion are over sixty. Because of these demographic facts, the communities are bound to increase in size over the next twenty years, both absolutely and relatively. It has been estimated that the Pakistani heritage population will eventually stabilise towards the year 2020 at about 1,250,000. At the time of the 2001 census, it was 747,285.

The percentages in the right hand column of Table 1 are shown in graphic form in Figure 1.

2 IF HE DOESN'T LOOK DEEPLY AT HIMSELF

Pressures and choices for the young

SUMMARY

This chapter describes how young British Pakistanis and Kashmiris, like all other young British people, seek and shape their identities within a range of influences and pressures. Some of the influences are mutually compatible but others are in conflict and young people are pulled in opposite directions. There are notes here about family life; the mosque and mosque-based education; new developments in Islamic theology and spirituality; street culture and youth culture; and currents of thought and influence loosely known as 'fundamentalism'.

Overview

'My worries are,' says the father of Tanveer, a Year 9 student, 'next two years, if he doesn't look deeply at himself, what he's doing, he's going to miss the opportunity of a lifetime.' Young British Pakistanis, like all other young British people, seek and shape their identities within a range of influences and pressures. Some of the influences are mutually compatible and they therefore reinforce each other. Others, however, are in conflict and young people are pulled in opposite directions. Tanveer's parents, like all parents, fear that he won't manage the conflicts with optimum success. There are notes in this chapter about some of the poles towards which young British Pakistani people may be attracted, and from which they may be repelled:

- [ ] family life

- [ ] the mosque and mosque-based education

- [ ] new developments in Islamic theology and spirituality

- [ ] street culture and youth culture

- [ ] currents of thought and influence variously known as 'fundamentalism' or 'political Islam'.

Also, schools exert enormous influence, both attractive and repelling. This point is introduced in chapter 3 and is discussed in its many facets throughout chapters 4-11.

Some of the difficulties of navigating between different pulls and pushes are evoked in Tariq Mehmood's novel *While there is Light*, published in 2003. The main character came from Pakistan to live in Bradford when he was a child. As an adult he returns for a visit to Pakistan. 'I thought I understood the world,' he says to himself (in English) at one stage. 'But ... I am nothing more than *Valaiti-babu*, a *gora* [white man] imprisoned in the skin of a Paki. A Paki in England, unwanted. A *Valaiti* [Britisher] in Pakistan, naive, arrogant, despicable.'

Family life

Three groups of Year 6 Pakistani heritage pupils in a northern city were asked what they thought their parents wanted for them in later life. The full range of their replies is illustrated with the following phrases:

- [ ] get a good report
- [ ] do well in football or cricket
- [ ] be good
- [ ] be a doctor or nurse
- [ ] have good luck
- [ ] get good GCSEs and a good job
- [ ] be good at work
- [ ] be sorted.

Children from other ethnic backgrounds were also included in the interviews. Their answers were virtually identical, except that there was reference amongst white children to having boyfriends and girlfriends, and to 'being best'. But basically, the point is, Pakistani heritage parents have the same high aspirations and expectations for their children as do all parents. This was illustrated in interviews with parents of Year 9 learners. Shazad's mother said: 'I want him to go to university, achieve his goals and be happy in life. It's a self-fulfilling prophecy, you expect him to achieve and so he does. Sometimes they say to me 'You expect us to be so perfect', and I say 'You can, you can!''

Year 9 learners themselves said:

☐ Parents used to tell us 'We didn't do that good at school, and we hope you do', and we used to just laugh, thinking it's funny – but now we're older and wiser.

☐ They just want me to do really good, and they go 'Whatever you want to do, we'll always be behind you'.

Pakistani families, like all families, vary in their approaches to bringing up children and in the boundaries and constraints they place on, and the freedoms they permit to, teenagers. But young British Pakistanis, like all young people at all times and in all places, may be impatient or critical about some of their parents' loyalties and priorities.

Monica Ali's novel *Brick Lane* is about a Bangladeshi-heritage family, not a Pakistani one. But many young British Pakistani people will recognise the kinds of tension that the novel affectionately but poignantly explores, not least since British Pakistanis and British Bangladeshis have in common the Islamic religion. There are tensions between parents and teenagers, between sisters, between father and mother; and between home and school, home and street, home and community. There is an extract from the novel in box 3. The extract shows how the dynamics that exist in all families in all cultures may be played out in one particular family in one particular place and context.

The mosque

Up to the age of 14 most British Pakistani children attend a local mosque school. The pedagogical style is typically different from that which they encounter at their mainstream school, for it puts much emphasis on learning the Qur'an in Arabic by heart and on oral repetition (*tartil/tajwid*), and gives relatively low

---

Box 3

What's the wrong with you?
– a glimpse of family dynamics

Chanu, the head of the household, has accessed a Bangladeshi website on his computer. He calls his teenage daughters to look at it. One, Bibi, dutifully does so. The other, Shahana, declines. The mother, Nazneen, tries to be a peacemaker. Shahana, by the way, has recently developed the mannerism of blowing at her fringe. Rightly or wrongly, her father interprets this as insolence.

'Bangla2000 web site. Who wants to take a look?'

Bibi stepped closer to her father. But he was waiting for Shahana. Nazneen put her hand on Shahana's arm. 'Go on, girl,' she whispered. Shahana did not budge. 'Take a little look.'

'No. It's bor-ing.'

Chanu jumped up and turned round in one movement so that the dining chair toppled. His cheeks quivered. 'Too boring for the memsahib?'

'She's going to look now,' said Nazneen. Bibi backed away from her father, a barely perceptible shuffling that gave the impression that she was responding to the tug of her mother's force field.

'What is the wrong with you?' shouted Chanu, speaking in English.

'Do you mean,' said Shahana, ''What is wrong with you?' She blew at her fringe. 'Not 'the wrong'.'

He gasped hard as if she had punched him in the stomach. For a few seconds his jaw worked frantically. 'Tell your sister,' he screamed, reverting to Bengali, ...

---

priority, in the first instance, to discussion and intellectual understanding. The imams and other teachers at the mosque schools mostly received their own education, both secular and religious, outside Britain. There is an increasingly widespread perception in Muslim communities that such imams are not equipped by their own training to help young British Pakistanis cope with issues such as unemployment, racism and Islamophobia, drugs and drug-dealing, and the attractions of Western youth culture. Box 4 contains a description of mosque-based education in

Box 4

Generation gap – issues and concerns in mosques

The growth of Muslims in Britain has created in some ways a generation gap. In the early days of migration and settlement, Muslims imported imams to run their local mosques and teach their children basic Islamic education. The imams presumed that the children they were teaching in the mosques and madrasahs were the children of Mirpuris, Punjabis or Bengalis and treated them as such. But the reality was different.

During the day the children were encouraged to question and reason but the same children, in their evening classes in the mosques, were discouraged from questioning and reasoning. Rather, the emphasis was on repeating and memorising. A child perhaps wants to know the reason behind what she or he is learning, but this was something the imams invariably discouraged. Furthermore, the children's language of communication has increasingly become English, and now for the third generation of Muslims, English is their first language. But in a large number of madrasahs the imams still teach them in Urdu, or in other Asian languages. It is not surprising that there is an increasing frustration amongst the youth about such methods of teaching.

The increasing use of imams from villages of the Indian sub-continent and the reliance of the congregation of a mosque on day-to-day *fiqh* issues seems, then, a problem rather than a cure. ... The jurisprudential issues of living in Britain have hardly been touched upon by imams, nor do they think there is an urgency to do so. They lead daily prayers, they conduct marriages, lead *janazah* (funeral) prayers and perform similar other requirements of the congregation.

However, very few possess the skills and the vision to understand the meaning of living as a Muslim in a pluralist society. The community has recognised this gap and opened up seminaries to train their imams. But the tragedy is that the syllabus of such seminaries hardly reflects contemporary challenges and needs. The only difference between an imported imam and a local trained imam lies in the fact that the latter can convey his message in English, whilst the former cannot.

Source: Ataullah Siddiqui, Muslims in Britain Past and Present, Islam Today, 1995

the mid 1990s and summarises the concerns which many Muslim observers continue to have.

New developments in Muslim theology and spirituality

There are several national and local organisations which seek to promote understanding of the Muslim faith within the setting of a non-Muslim country such as Britain. Their publications and extensive websites are in English, as are the meetings they organise. In addition to seeking to develop a Muslim theology and lifestyle suitable for non-Muslim settings they provide information and resources about Islam for society at large. The aspirations of such groups were succinctly summarised in an editorial in the magazine *Q News* in autumn 2003. There is an extract in box 5.

Amongst other things, the development of a British form of Islam – or, more widely, a European or western form of Islam – involves re-considering the traditional pedagogy of mosque-based education, and the theories of knowledge, learning and spirituality that

underlie it. The need for such review was alluded to in box 4. It is outlined also in box 6.

Islamophobia

Islamophobia is a new word in the English language. It was first used in print in 1991 and became widely known after the publication in 1997 of a Runnymede Trust report. The report defined it as 'unfounded hostility towards Islam, and therefore fear or dislike of all or most Muslims'.

Hostility towards Islam and Muslims has been a feature of European societies since the Crusades. It has taken different forms, however, at different times and in different circumstances and it has fulfilled a variety of functions. It may be more apt to speak of 'Islamophobias' rather than of a single phenomenon. Each version of Islamophobia has its own features as well as similarities with, and borrowings from, other versions. A key factor since the 1960s is the presence of some fifteen million Muslim people in western European countries. Another is the increased power on

---

Box 5

A critical phase in history
– the development of a British form of Islam

We are in a critical phase in history in the development of a British form of Islam. The process is bound to be painful and strenuous but it must, and is, taking place. And it is happening in all sorts of places – in the internet cafes, around the local youth hangouts, within the mosques and in-between prayers, among mini-cab drivers, city professionals, social workers, teachers, kebab sellers – everywhere the demand is to identify and embrace aspects of our faith that have immediate relevancy to our own identities, spiritual or otherwise.

Our intention at *Q* has always been to be a window to this dynamic process: to report, comment and analyse all that is taking place without being either judgemental or aloof. The debate is too serious, too exciting to be partisan about. Nevertheless it demands frontline engagement and we have tried on several occasions to provide this.

But now our experimentation of British Islam seems destined to have a greater influence globally. Britain's history, its spiritual landscape, central location vis-à-vis the Muslim world, the nature and composition of its Muslim population, the English language, are all pointing to a unique development.

Is it right at this moment to argue that the prototype of the kind of Islam relevant to the twenty-first century will evolve within the British environment? Are we to be the leading global exporter of a kind of Islam that will truly reflect the great ethos of the faith, a kind of Islam that is relevant for our times – at ease with itself in the global village?

Source: editorial in Q News, autumn 2003

Box 6

What happened?
– the need for independent reasoning

The major question that Western Muslims ask – and will ask even more insistently when the school system effectively acknowledges the debt we all owe to Muslim scholarship – and that perplexes many writers and scholars is this: what happened? What happened to Islam that led to its decline, to its rude shocks when the military vanguards of another and alien culture defeated it so comprehensively over such a long period of time?

The answer is as complex as the question is simple. Huge tomes and learned treatises relate the decline of the Islamic civilisation to a diverse range of economic, industrial, military and other causes. For educationalists, however, one of the key factors appears to have been the alleged ending of *ijtihad*, normally translated as independent reasoning or thinking.

Over time scholars have argued for restoration of *ijtihad* as the means of rejuvenating Muslim civilisation. The restoration movement itself gathered serious pace over 200 hundred years ago. Certain scholars at that time were extremely critical of knowledge acquired by heart and assessed without any concern for interpretation and understanding. The tradition of memorising, it was argued, was no longer able to fit the modern era for which is needed, in addition to the religious matter, analytical knowledge, comprehension and, moreover, contextualisation. This is not just an esoteric debate, for it goes to the very heart of western Muslims' attempt to locate themselves as western Muslims, and to the pedagogical style that many Muslims undergo at the *madrasahs*.

Source: adapted slightly from a paper by Maurice Irfan Coles, 2003

---

the world stage of oil-rich countries, many of which are Islamic in their culture and traditions. A third is the emergence of repressive regimes, and of political movements that use terrorist tactics to achieve their aims, which claim to be motivated and justified by Islamic beliefs. The latter have had a hugely greater profile since 11 September 2001.

The features of anti-Muslim hostility in modern Britain are summarised in Box 7.

The cumulative effect of the features listed in Box 7 is that Muslims are made to feel that they do not truly belong here – they feel that they are not truly accepted, let alone welcomed, as full members of British society. On the contrary, they are seen as 'an enemy within' or 'a fifth column'. This is bad for society as well as for

Box 7

A new word for an old fear
– the features of Islamophobia

- Verbal and physical attacks on Muslims in public places
- Attacks on mosques and desecration of Muslim cemeteries
- Widespread and routine negative stereotypes in the media, including the broadsheets, and in the conversations and 'common sense' of non-Muslims – people talk and write about Muslims in ways that would not be acceptable if the reference were to Jewish people, for example, or to black people
- Discrimination in recruitment and employment practices, and in workplace cultures and customs
- Bureaucratic delay and inertia in responding to Muslim requests for cultural sensitivity in education and healthcare and in planning applications for mosques
- Lack of attention to the fact that Muslims in Britain are disproportionately affected by poverty and social exclusion
- Non-recognition of Muslims in particular, and of religion in general, by the law of the land, since up until recently discrimination in employment on grounds of religion has been lawful and discrimination in the provision of services is still lawful
- Anomalies in public order legislation, such that Muslims are less protected against incitement to hatred than members of certain other religions
- Laws curtailing civil liberties that disproportionately affect Muslims.

Source: Islamophobia: issues, challenges and action, *Trentham Books, 2004*

Muslims themselves. Both Muslim and non-Muslim commentators have pointed out that a young generation of British Muslims is developing who feel increasingly disaffected, alienated and bitter.

'The most subtle and for Muslims perilous consequence of Islamophobic actions,' a Muslim scholar has observed, 'is the silencing of self-criticism and the slide into defending the indefensible. Muslims decline to be openly critical of fellow Muslims, their ideas, activities and rhetoric in mixed company, lest this be seen as giving aid and comfort to the extensive forces of condemnation. Brotherhood, fellow feeling, sisterhood are genuine and authentic reflexes of Islam. But Islam is supremely a critical, reasoning and ethical framework, a system of values applicable first and foremost to Muslims. Islam cannot, or rather ought not, to be manipulated into 'my fellow Muslim right or wrong'.' She goes on to observe that Islamophobia provides 'the perfect rationale for modern Muslims to become reactive, addicted to a culture of complaint and blame that serves only to increase the powerlessness, impotence and frustration of being a Muslim.'[1]

Islamophobia can have the effect of undermining young people's self-confidence and self-esteem, their confidence in their parents and families, and their respect for Islam. It makes extremist organisations, however, attractive in ways that they wouldn't be otherwise. An editorial article in a Muslim periodical has put the point as follows:

> For many youngsters, Islam is proving to be a genuine way out, a way to make sense of the bewildering maelstrom of currents surrounding them. For many others, it is a reactionary grab at something they see as a source of opposition. The irony is that by demonising Muslims the mass media is also erecting a romantic notion of opposition to mainstream culture.[2]

Street culture, youth culture and 'fundamentalism'

Older Muslims as well as non-Muslims are deeply concerned about what is happening in British society to young Muslim men, particularly those of Pakistani, Kashmiri and Bangladeshi heritage. A Muslim observer comments as follows:

> The parents of these young men neglected their religious training, and instead left matters in the hands of the madrasahs. Their experience in the madrasah has been of rote learning without any understanding, an experience that has left them bored and alienated not only from the madrasah but also from religion itself. Frustrated imams throw the more disruptive kids out of the madrasahs onto the streets. Clubbing together in

gangs of around 20-30, these young men are listless and bored. The result has very often been the emergence of gang violence and turf wars. 'Islam is drab and boring,' they say, 'it is only about things you are not allowed to do. There is no fun and laughter. We are young and now is the time for enjoyment.'

'This is not just a problem of young Muslim men who have lost their way,' he continues, 'but a failure of the whole community to bring them up with Islamic values. We have neglected their spiritual training (*tarbiya*) and failed to teach them how to live in this world in accordance with the pleasure of Allah (*akhlaqiyyat*) in a way that makes sense to them. We have even ignored their secular education; so that, on the streets of despair, turning to drugs seems the best way to make a quick buck or to escape from the pressures of racism, Islamophobia and unemployment.' There is a further extract from this author in box 8.

'We laugh along with Ali G, writes another Muslim observer, 'because he is everything we do not wish our kids to be, yet see evidence of daily... The species of nominal Muslim Ali G is meant to represent [is] typically unemployed and poorly educated, he is the type who sees a brighter future in taking on the trappings of the LA 'gangsta' rather than the uncool and 'foreign' traditions of his parents... The character gives the lie to the sound bite that Islam is Britain's fastest growing religion...The British Muslim community is haemorrhaging.'[3]

A sociologist who studied young British Pakistani males in the 1990s in Birmingham, Bradford and London reported that 'Islam.... plays a role in the construction of masculinity ... a 'hard' image of tough aggressive macho men.' He mentioned that the youths claimed membership of Hamas or Hizb-ut-Tahrir yet were unaware who Shias were, and how they differed from Sunnis, and did not know what Hamas or Hizb-ut-Tahrir actually represented. They would daub walls with the slogan 'Hamas Rules OK', and support antisemitic, homophobic and misogynist organisations such as Hizb-ut-Tahrir, but this was more an act of rebellion and defiance than to do with the rise of so-called fundamentalism.[4]

It is all, he said, about being 'hard'. Islamic terms such as Hamas, Hizb-ut-Tahrir or Tablighi Jamaat were not

---

Box 8

Negative Masculinity
A spiritual problem

Negative masculinity occurs when a youth misuses his natural qualities of enthusiasm, strength and bravery ... He thinks it is cool to follow the lifestyles of the street, and at the rough end this means getting involved in crime. What is even worse, as one young brother said to me recently, is that as corrupt lifestyles become widespread among Muslim youth, it becomes harder for younger teenagers to see the straight path...The negative role models closest to hand now come from within our own community.

Negative masculinity is about showing off, about trying to be 'hard', and about using physical strength to humiliate others. The fake man thinks strength should be used to dominate others so that he gets 'nuff respect' from his peers and enemies out of a sense of fear...

Negative masculinity is about the obsession to have the right 'look': the designer clothes, the most up-to-date mobile phone, the latest trainers, and the flashiest car... [It] is about wasting time and playing around like a child ... He looks out for himself first, neither respecting the wishes of his parents nor serving them, and ignoring the needs of others around him. Many of the criminalised gangs rob and prey on the weakest members of their own community. Instead of being the pride of the community, these lost young men have become its badge of shame.

Negative masculinity is about being a slave to desire. The signs of this slavery are the impulse for instant gratification and the immediate feeling of frustration and anger when desire is not quickly satiated. Servitude to caprice entraps the slave in a cage of restless discontent. Why? Because if we want the latest fashion, one thing can be sure, it will go out of date.

In short, the problem of negative masculinity is a spiritual one.

Source: Being a Real Man in Islam by Yahya Birt (2001)

---

used with knowledge of what the words stood for but as badges and markers in various kinds of turf war and battles to control pieces of urban space. (In an analogous way, it has been pointed out, some of the supporters of a football team – Millwall is sometimes mentioned in this context – use their team's colours and emblems as markers of identity over and against others on the streets rather than to signal deep allegiance to a specific club.)

Extremist organisations and websites in Britain are frequently anti-western and their references to Judaism and Israel are often indistinguishable from crude antisemitism. Their hostility to all things western is a mirror image of western Islamophobia and indeed helps to feed it. Their simplistic messages can be attractive to young people, however, since they appear at first sight to give a satisfactory picture of the total world situation (the West is the root of all evil) and appear to have a clear practical agenda (resistance and

struggle). They have far fewer active supporters than the mainstream media claim. The support they do have, as mentioned in some of the quotations above, and as illustrated in the article quoted in box 9, may reflect a young man's search for identity in a hostile world rather than a carefully thought through commitment.

School
The lack of educational achievement amongst some young British Muslims is a matter of great concern, as are the unemployment and alienation to which it leads. The next chapter discusses the extent and nature of the under-achievement and thus prepares the way for the next main section of the book.

Box 9

They're our role models – the posturing of youth

A reporter from The Times *listens in on a conversation in Keighley between a British-Pakistani youth worker, Amjad Zaman, and some 16-year-old youths.*

'Some of the older boys are forming a mujaheddin group,' said 16-year-old Ansar. 'They're our role models, the Afghans.' Another Asian teenager claims that Osama bin Laden, the alleged terrorist mastermind, is his hero, but Amjad Zaman told both of them, in a Yorkshire accent as strong as theirs: 'Stop talking such nonsense. You're just making it up.' We are in West Yorkshire. Devonshire Park in Keighley, to be precise, not central Asia, and it is easy to understand Mr Zaman's impatience with the posturing of youths who would get the shock of their lives if they ever met their supposed Taliban mentors.

The Islamic zealots who run Afghanistan might want to know, for example, how these unemployed young men came by their designer sportswear, let alone the car radio being passed around. But Mr Zaman nodded in agreement when the talk turns to the recent violence in Oldham, and 21-year-old Shihab said: 'We are going to stand our ground. If anyone comes to this park looking for trouble, we're not going to phone the police, we're going to mash them ourselves. They think that because they did it to our parents, they can do it to us, but that's where they're wrong.'

Devonshire Park looks well maintained, but immediately outside there are drifts of shattered car glass and discarded syringes. Ansar and his friends, second- and third-generation British-Pakistanis aged from 15 to 23, spend their afternoons here, playing cricket or football. Nearly all are past or current pupils of Greenhead secondary school, where Mr Zaman helps pupils with learning difficulties, but for some, attendance is mainly theoretical. One youth claims racism keeps him away, but again he gets short shrift from the older man. 'If you turn up at 11am and get excluded, that's your own fault,' he said. 'That's not racism.'

It is clear that Oldham is not an isolated case. All along the M62 there are depressed towns where white and Asian communities are retreating into a form of apartheid. Daily friction is reduced by greater separation, but flare-ups, when they come, are bigger. 'For me,' said Shihab, 'contact with whites means only one thing: trouble.' Older Asians are disturbed. 'Some of these people want to create a little Pakistan or Bangladesh,' said Mohammed Sharif, a 41-year-old NHS worker in Keighley. 'They don't want to mix with whites, because they see them as a bad, un-Islamic influence, but they say they wouldn't want to live in Pakistan either. My generation felt a bit the same way, but we still respected our elders. We have no control over these young people.'

Source: article by Raymond Whitaker in The Times, *17 June 2001*

A video short depicts a young man wearing a cap and a sweatshirt with a star and crescent on the back. Noticing the word 'PAKI' scrawled on a brick wall, he walks away in the direction he came from and returns with a marker. Above the graffiti he writes his own: 'PROUD 2 B A'. Then he adds an exclamation mark after 'PAKI' and underlines the word itself. After standing back to look at his work he leaves.

The video was created in 2003 as part of an advertisement for a clothing business based in Peterborough. Early in 2004, there was substantial media coverage about it and about the controversy it aroused.

Some feared it would provoke a backlash; some disapproved of all graffiti as irresponsible and disrespectful; some felt the video legitimised racist name-calling. Defenders of the video maintained it was reclaiming a racist term in order to assert the dignity of British Pakistani identity. 'The racists hijacked this word and the power and confidence is with them,' explained businessman Abdul Rahim. 'I want that power and confidence back with us.'

The character in the video was dressed in Western street-culture clothes, and wrote in digital shorthand, in order to evoke the context in which his act of antiracist self-definition took place. One way of opposing racism, the video implied, is to endow racist language and imagery with positive, self-affirming meaning.

The controversy aroused by the video was a debate also about the multiple identities and affiliations of British Pakistani young people.

3 LIFE CHANCES
Achievement and progress in the education system

SUMMARY

This chapter reviews statistical evidence from the period 1990-2003 relating to the academic progress and achievement of British-Pakistani learners in schools. Overall, Pakistani-heritage learners are achieving below national averages, though differentials vary at different ages and between different local authorities. It is noted that British-Pakistani families and households are disproportionately affected by poverty and social exclusion. For example, nearly 40 per cent of all Pakistani-heritage learners in secondary schools are affected by poverty, as measured by eligibility for free school meals, compared with a national average of fewer than 20 per cent. The implications of this are considered.

Commitments and statistics

'As a Pakistani teacher educated in England,' writes someone who took part in the compilation of this book, 'I share many of the experiences of the children I am now supporting. In the mothers who come to school with their children, I recognise my own mother. It took me a degree and a teacher training qualification to appreciate the messages I will be giving them. They will need time.'

It is an inspiring statement of personal and professional commitment. Also, it is a reminder of one of the functions of education. Becoming educated is not just a matter of acquiring qualifications and improved life-chances, valuable as these certainly are. It is a matter too of acquiring insights into one's own history and social location, of reflecting on the personal and professional responsibilities that educational qualifications bestow, and of developing wisdom and knowledge to pass on to the next generation, and the skills with which to do it.

Other chapters in this book deal with issues of identity, responsibility and involvement in wider society. In this chapter the focus is on the collection, analysis and interpretation of statistics about achievement.

National sources of information about levels of educational achievement in Pakistani heritage communities include the Youth Cohort Study (YCS), the Pupil Level Annual Schools Census (PLASC), the Universities and Colleges Admissions Service (UCAS) and the Labour Force Survey (LFS). Locally and in certain respects more valuably, there are reports and papers published as committee papers in local education authorities. This chapter begins by reviewing the evidence from national sources. It then considers data about poverty and social exclusion affecting British Pakistani communities. It closes by discussing briefly the implications and tasks for schools and by introducing the next main part of this book.

A word of caution before the chapter gets under way. All statistics currently available use the term 'Pakistani' without distinguishing between the different groups to which this generic term refers. In fact, as stressed in chapter 1, the Pakistani community in Britain is a community of communities. Statistics about the total community are not necessarily accurate about particular parts, for example the Kashmiri community.

Youth Cohort Study

Until 2003 the YCS was the only national source of information about the achievement of Pakistani heritage pupils at school. Run under the auspices of the DfES, it is a major programme of longitudinal research that looks at young people's education, employment

LIFE CHANGES

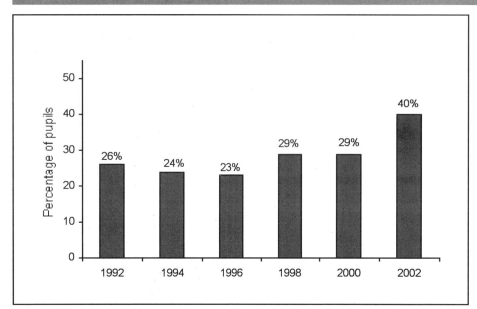

Figure 2: Attainment at 16+ by Pakistani-heritage pupils 1992-2002 (Source YCS February 2003)

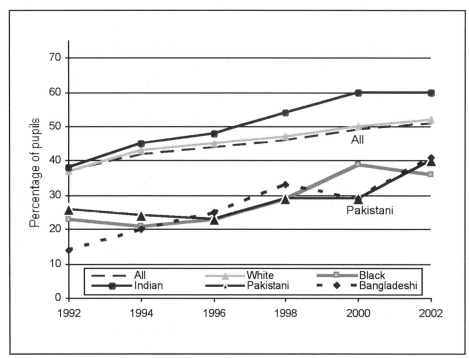

Figure 3: Attainment at 16+ by ethnicity 1992-2002 (Source YCS February 2003)

experience, training and qualifications. It involves study of a representative sample of young people following completion of compulsory education and again one and two years later. It has collected information concerning young people of Pakistani heritage since 1992, although until recently did not distinguish in its reporting between Pakistani and Bangladeshi young people.

In February 2003, the YCS published the attainment of five A*-C grades at GCSE of young people in all cohorts from 1992 to 2002 by ethnicity. This showed that in 1992 only 26 per cent of Pakistani heritage

pupils achieved this level, compared with 37 per cent of white pupils and 38 per cent of Indian-heritage pupils. Between 1992 and 2002 there was a rise in achievement of young people from all communities but there was a significant gap each year between the performance of Pakistani heritage pupils and the national average. The gap widened through the 1990s, as shown in Figure 1. It narrowed strikingly, however, in 2002 and the improvement was maintained in 2003.

It was not possible during the 1990s to draw firm conclusions from YCS data about the attainment of Pakistani heritage pupils nationally, nor to study the

Figure 4: Attainment at 16+ by ethnicity, summer 2002 (Source NPD 2002)

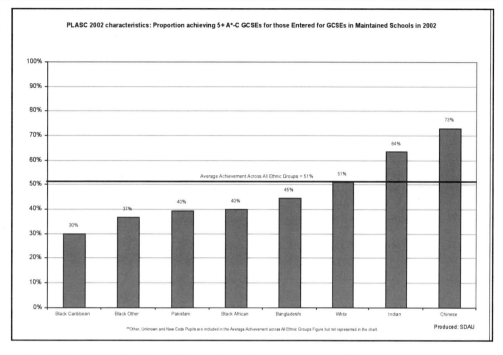

PLASC 2002 characteristics: Proportion achieving 5+ A*-C GCSEs for those Entered for GCSEs in Maintained Schools in 2002

Average Achievement Across All Ethnic Groups = 51%

Produced: SDAU

Figure 5: Attainment at 16+ by ethnicity, summer 2003 (Source PLASC Data 2003 Provisional)

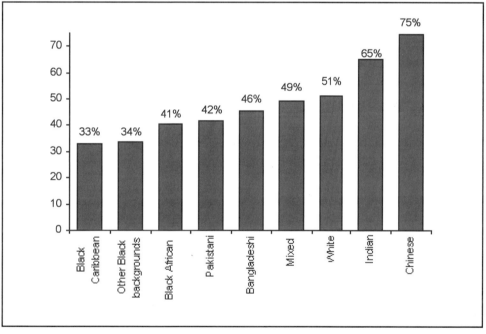

attainment of pupils as they progress through the education system. This changed with the introduction of the Pupil Level Annual Schools' Census (PLASC) in January 2002. This is an annual census that involves collecting information on every individual pupil in maintained schools with regard to ethnicity, eligibility for free school meals, special educational needs (SEN), and English as an additional language (EAL) in such a way that it can be linked to attainment data. The first national data concerning the attainment of pupils from different ethnic groups was published in 2003 and related to results from summer 2002. A year later results were published for summer 2003. Figures 4 and 5 show the overall picture for each of the two years. The attainment of Pakistani heritage students rose between the two years but so did that of most other groups. The gap between Pakistani achievement and the national average did not narrow.

Figures 2-5 show the big picture, but are unhelpful insofar as they obscure differences of gender, social class, first language, stage of schooling and location

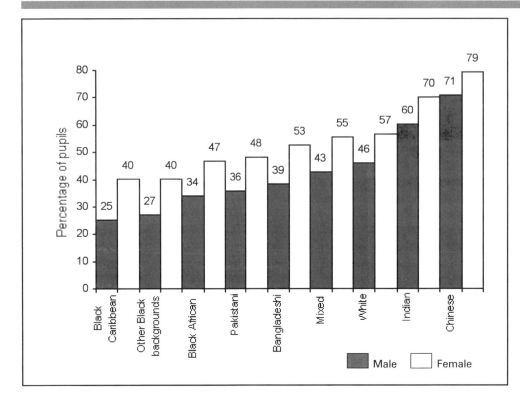

Figure 6: Attainment at 16+ by ethnicity and gender, summer 2003 (Source PLASC Data 2003 Provisional)

within England, and the key differences between the Pakistani community in general and Kashmiri communities in particular.

Gender

PLASC data shows that in all communities at GCSE the results of girls are better than those of boys. In summer 2003, for example, 48 per cent of Pakistani heritage girls achieved five A*-C grades, but only 36 per cent of Pakistani boys (see Figure 6). This differential was slightly larger than the gender differential amongst white, Indian and Chinese students.

The gap between Pakistani heritage girls and boys is different in different subjects. This is shown strikingly in Figure 7. At key stages 1-3 girls outperform boys in English, reading and writing. But there is no significant variation between girls and boys at any age in mathematics and science.

Progress

It is crucial to consider not only how well pupils achieved but also how well they achieved in relation to their previous attainment. This information not only sheds light on the impact of schooling on young people, but also illustrates the potential of young people to achieve at even higher levels than they do.

The first national report[1] to relate the attainment of pupils at each key stage to their attainment in the preceding stage shows with regard to Pakistani heritage pupils the following points:

☐ At KS2, Pakistani heritage pupils made poor progress in mathematics and science and this affected boys and girls equally

☐ At KS3 they made average progress in English but below average progress in mathematics and science

☐ At GCSE they progressed very well, falling just behind the top three groups in terms of pupil progress

☐ Pakistani heritage boys made average progress throughout school

☐ Pakistani heritage girls did not progress well at KS 2; at KS3 their progress was average; at GCSE it was far above average.

Figure 7: Attainment of Pakistani-heritage pupils by gender and stage of schooling, summer 2003 (Source PLASC Data 2003 Provisional)

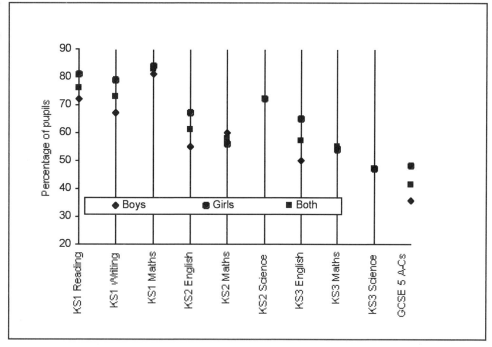

There is an urgent need for further research here. What are the factors that contribute to the remarkable progress made by Pakistani heritage girls between KS3 and GCSE? To what extent are there lessons to be learnt that are applicable to Pakistani heritage boys?

English as an additional language

Along with gender and socio-economic circumstance, it is important to recognise the influence of having English as an additional language (EAL) on attainment and, more particularly, on progress. Most Pakistani heritage pupils are classified for PLASC purposes as having EAL. Unfortunately, the classification provides no information concerning how well pupils can speak or write in English in different situations or for different purposes, nor valuable information about their first language and how proficient they are in it. The classification merely records the fact that the first language that the child was exposed to was not English or, in some cases, 'believed not to be English'.

PLASC data indicates that the relatively small group of Pakistani heritage pupils who speak English as a first language attain at significantly higher levels in all areas. This is almost certainly connected with social class rather than with language alone. The crude English/not English categorisation limits the usefulness of analysis of EAL as a factor in attainment, although much stronger data related to language levels often exists locally. It is well established through long term research that to achieve academic language fluency in a second language takes at least five to seven years, and that it is often in subject-specific areas that academic language fluency is most difficult to achieve. The gradual nature of the development of academic language proficiency may help to explain the picture of considerable progress made in the later stages of education and the relative lack of progress in mathematics and science.

Regional differences

There is substantial variation of pupil attainment around the country. In London, for example, Pakistani heritage pupils attained at levels above both the regional and national averages in 2003 (see table 2). Regional variations in Pakistani heritage attainment are much greater than regional variations in the attainment of all pupils. It is likely that this reflects the differing material circumstances, social class profiles and migration histories of different Pakistani communities rather than the quality of educational provision. It is significant in this respect that London is not one of the principal places of Kashmiri settlement.

	Number of Pakistani heritage 16 year olds in 2003	Percentage of Pakistani heritage boys achieving 5 A*-C in 2003	Percentage of Pakistani heritage girls achieving 5 A*-C in 2003	Percentage of all Pakistani heritage pupils achieving 5 A*-C in 2003	Percentage of all pupils achieving 5 A*-C in 2003	Difference between Pakistani heritage and regional average
North East	246	33.6	47.9	40.7	46.6	-5.9
North West	2,262	35.2	47.6	41.0	49.1	-8.1
Yorkshire and the Humber	3,016	29.1	39.4	34.0	45.4	-11.4
East Midlands	527	44.8	50.2	47.4	50.4	-3.0
West Midlands	2,990	34.3	48.9	41.0	49.9	-8.9
East of England	734	35.1	46.0	40.5	53.8	-13.3
London	2,346	47.4	58.7	52.8	50.2	2.6
South East	1,147	36.8	52.5	44.0	55.1	-11.1
South West	101	24.6	47.7	34.7	54.4	-19.7

Source PLASC 2003

Table 2: Attainment of Pakistani heritage students at 16+ by region, 2003

There is further information about regional variations in table 3. The table lists the 19 LEAs with the largest numbers of Pakistani heritage pupils at 16+ in 2003 and shows that there were substantial differences between authorities with regard to:

☐ Attainment – the range was from 28 per cent of Pakistani heritage students gaining higher grades in one LEA to 61 per cent in another

☐ Improvement – the range of improvement between 2002 and 2003 was from +9 percentage points in one LEA to -6 in another

☐ Differentials – the differential between Pakistani heritage attainment and the LEA average ranged from +9 in one LEA to -24 in another.

Pathways after the age of 16
Information from the Youth Cohort Study indicates that whilst 77 per cent of Pakistani heritage young people go on to further study, Pakistani young people are less likely to be in full time employment or in government sponsored training, and more likely to be unemployed, than young people as a whole.

UCAS has monitored applications and admissions to higher education by ethnicity since 1994. It collects and publishes data on the regions from which students come, the locations and types of university to which they go, and the types and levels of qualifications they have gained at school.

The first thing to stress from the data is that Pakistani heritage young people, both male and female, are well represented statistically in higher education, and indeed they are better represented than might be expected from estimates of their numbers in the age-group to which they belong. For example, it has been estimated that they are about 1.7 per cent of their age group whereas they constitute 2.4 per cent of first year students.[2]

	Number of Pakistani heritage 16 year olds in 2003	Percentage of Pakistani heritage 16 year olds achieving 5 A*-C in 2002	Percentage of Pakistani heritage 16 year olds achieving 5 A*-C in 2003	Change in Pakistani heritage 16 year olds achieving 5 A*-C 2002 – 2003 (percentage points)	LEA average of 16 year olds achieving 5 A*-C in 2003	Difference between Pakistani heritage and LEA average achieving 5 A*-C in 2003
Birmingham	1,983	38.1	43.0	4.9	48.8	-5.8
Blackburn with Darwen	262	34.7	28.6	-6.1	38.7	-10.1
Bradford	1,393	28.1	30.2	2.1	39.4	-9.2
Buckinghamshire	317	36.3	40.4	4.1	65.2	-24.8
Calderdale	221	37.1	46.6	9.5	51.9	-5.3
City of Nottingham	202	33.2	37.3	4.1	34.8	2.5
Ealing	212	53.3	48.4	-4.9	53.9	-5.5
Kirklees	492	37.0	37.8	0.8	47.0	-9.2
Lancashire	616	38.5	41.3	2.8	53.0	-11.7
Leeds	372	25.8	33.4	7.6	44.2	-10.8
Luton	419	38.7	38.2	-0.5	41.3	-3.1
Manchester	457	40.0	48.4	8.4	39.2	9.2
Newham	417	39.1	46.4	7.3	45.7	0.7
Oldham	272	26.5	33.7	7.2	44.3	-10.6
Redbridge	266	56.0	61.5	5.5	65.4	-3.9
Rochdale	379	42.0	37.7	-4.3	41.2	-3.5
Sheffield	270	24.1	30.7	6.6	43.0	-12.3
Slough	341	40.2	45.0	4.8	53.0	-8.0
Waltham Forest	418	47.6	49.6	2.0	44.9	4.7

Table 3: Attainment of Pakistani heritage pupils at 16+ in 19 LEAs, 2002 and 2003

Region	Number of Pakistani applicants	Proportion of Pakistani applicants*	Distribution of Pakistani pupils in schools	Difference
North East	160	1.9	1.7	+ .2
North West	1478	17.4	16.8	+ .6
Yorkshire and Humber	1555	18.3	22.6	- 4.3
East Midlands	357	4.2	3.9	+ .3
West Midlands	1531	18.0	22,9	- 4.9
East	97	1.1	5.6	- 4.4
Greater London	2126	25.0	17.5	+ 7.5
South East	1098	12.9	8.3	+ 4.6
South West	83	1.0	0.7	+ .3
	8485	(100)	100	

Source: UCAS 1999 and PLASC 2003.

* Column 3 provides a regional breakdown of the 8,485 applicants from Pakistani-heritage communities. The total does not add up quite to 100 per cent, since figures are provided to only one decimal point.

Table 4: Pakistani heritage applicants to British universities by region, 1999

At first sight, this finding appears to run counter to the findings of the YCS and PLASC concerning attainment at school. If Pakistani heritage students are less likely than others to achieve well at 16, how can they be so well represented at university? The explanation probably lies in the distinction between Pakistani and Kashmiri. Certainly this is suggested by a regional analysis of applicants of Pakistani heritage, for disproportionately high numbers of Pakistani applicants are from Greater London, East Anglia and the South East, which are not the principal places of Kashmiri settlement. This is shown in Table 4, which is based on the most recently published figures: the numbers of applicants in 1999 and the census of school population in 2003.

Table 4 shows that Pakistani applicants to universities are under-represented from the West Midlands and Yorkshire and Humber. In the case of London and the South East, however, they are over-represented. It may be reasonably speculated that the differences between regions are to do with material circumstances and social class profiles between different Pakistani communities, not with differing educational provision.

Social class

It is well-known that there is a close correlation in every society between educational attainment and social class. The correlation in England was re-stated in 2003 by, amongst others, the Cabinet Office Strategy Unit and Her Majesty's Chief Inspector of Schools. The Strategy Unit reported that in 2000 (the last year for which figures were available) 70 per cent of children of people in managerial and professional occupations achieved five A*-C grades at GCSE, compared with fewer than 30 per cent of children whose parents were in unskilled manual occupations. Further, the 40 percentage points difference between these groups had not changed since 1989.

The Chief Inspector considered changes and developments in England since the publication of a major Ofsted report in 1993, *Access and Achievement in Urban Education*. 'The evidence,' he said, 'leads me to say that there has been improvement, but not enough. We must look again, urgently, at how to close the gap in achievement between youngsters in deprived areas and elsewhere.' There are further extracts from his review in box 10. Incidentally, his remarks about avoiding both a blame culture and an excuse culture are extremely relevant in the present context of considering the attainment of pupils and students of Pakistani heritage.

LIFE CHANCES

Box 10

We must look again – problems in urban education

... The evidence leads me to say that there has been improvement, but not enough. We must look again, urgently, at how to close the gap in achievement between youngsters in deprived areas and elsewhere.'

... Progress in narrowing the gap in achievement has been slow.

... We examined schools in urban wards with high levels of deprivation. Currently there are about 850 primary and 150 secondary schools that serve areas of urban deprivation and have more than 35 per cent of their pupils entitled to free school meals. Of these, we have visited around 500 primary and 70 secondary schools at least twice, and at least once since January 2000.

... Analysis shows that improvement has been more marked in primary than secondary schools, but it has generally been slow and unsteady.

... Attainment in secondary schools serving deprived urban areas has improved since 1993. But less than a third of pupils in these schools leave with five or more good GCSEs, compared with about half in other schools. Compared with schools nationally, almost twice as many pupils from these schools leave without any GCSE certificates at all.

... Since 1996, the socio-economic attainment gap has narrowed in primary schools but it has widened somewhat in secondary schools. Generally, the gap is such that, by the age of 16 years, 81 per cent of pupils whose parents are in 'higher professional occupations' gain at least five good GCSE passes, compared with 32 per cent of pupils whose parents have what are defined as 'routine occupations'.

... But although progress is often frustratingly slow, we are now clear that there are two equal and opposite dangers to be avoided if the nettle is to be grasped firmly. On the one hand, there is absolutely no place for demonising those schools and those – adults and children – who work in them. This is not about a 'blame culture', castigating insensitively those who are tackling formidable challenges with resolution and commitment. But neither is there room for an 'excuse culture', a patronising or indulgent approach which condones low expectations or overstates the intractability of the external pressures.

... The fact that more schools are enabling more children to gain pleasure and a sense of achievement from education, as well as, potentially, power and control over their lives, is a cause for celebration. But that celebration will deserve to remain slightly muted until the still patchy and sporadic pattern of improvement becomes far more widespread and consistent. That is the challenge that faces us for the next ten years.

Source: speech by David Bell, Her Majesty's Chief Inspector of Schools, November 2003

It is an axiom of all statistical analysis that like may only ever be validly compared with like. It follows that statistics relating attainment with ethnicity are of limited validity and usefulness if they do not control the variable of social class. The PLASC-based charts printed above, for example, must be read with considerable caution, for the various communities to which they refer have different social class profiles – the charts do not compare like with like.

Data from the 2001 census, as also data from the Labour Force Survey over many years, shows that African-Caribbean, Pakistani and Bangladeshi communities are more likely than other communities to be affected by low pay, unemployment, under-employment, poor working conditions, poor health, overcrowded housing and poor-quality urban

environments. Their experience of material deprivation is compounded by racism on the streets and by institutional racism in the labour market and in public services and institutions. Some of the principal differences in material circumstances between Pakistani heritage households and white households are tabulated in table 5.

It is relevant to link the data in table 5 to a classification of British society proposed by a market research organisation. The classification is based on analysis of the 2001 census results and involves five categories: 'wealthy achievers', 'urban prosperous', 'comfortably off, 'moderate means' and 'hard pressed'. The data in table 5 indicates that there are likely to be very few Pakistani heritage households in the first two categories (wealthy achievers and urban prosperous)

Aspects of material circumstance	White communities	Pakistani heritage communities
Unemployment, all ages, both male and female,	4 per cent unemployment	16 per cent unemployment
Unemployment, males under 25	12 per cent unemployed	28 per cent unemployed
Proportion of income from wages and salaries	63 per cent	37 per cent
Proportion of income from benefits*	4 per cent	10 per cent
Proportion of households on low-income, before housing costs*	18.5 per cent	59 per cent
Proportion of households on low-income, before housing costs*	20.5 per cent	64 per cent
Health to		Three to four times more likely rate their health as bad or very bad than the general population
Entitlement to free school meals	15.6 per cent of pupils in primary schools, 12.3 per cent in secondary	32.5 per cent of pupils in primary schools, 38.3 per cent in secondary
Risk of being victim of a racist crime*	0.3 risk factor	4.2 risk factor

Notes

Items marked with an asterisk refer to both Pakistanis and Bangladeshis

All figures other than the one for free school meals (FSM) are from Social Focus in Brief produced by the Office of National Statistics in 2002 and are mostly derived from the Labour Force Survey. The FSM figure is from the DfES and relates to January 2003.

Table 5: Material circumstances of white and Pakistani communities compared

and that most are likely to be in the last two (moderate means or hard pressed). It is not the case, however, that they have a high proportion of one-parent households, or make much use of loans, or live in rented accommodation.

There is no data at present that cross-tabulates pupils' attainment with the categories proposed in Box 11, nor with the single most valid indicator of class, parental occupation. There is, however, data cross-tabulating data on attainment and entitlement to free school meals (FSM). The latter depends on a family being in receipt of income support or income-based job-seekers allowance. It is no more than a crude indicator for social class, therefore, since it merely distinguishes between the sixth of the school population who have the entitlement and the five sixths who do not. However, it is better than nothing.

As shown in table 5, over a third of all Pakistani heritage pupils are entitled to free school meals, compared with only 15 per cent of white pupils. It was not until 2003 that data on attainment, ethnicity and

entitlement to free school meals was published at national level. Three main points emerged:

☐ Within the British Pakistani community, as indeed within all communities, the attainment of pupils living in disadvantaged circumstances is lower than that of pupils who do not live in such circumstances: 46 per cent of non-FSM pupils of Pakistani heritage achieved five A*-C grades at GCSE in 2002, compared with only 33 per cent of FSM pupils.

☐ Pakistani heritage pupils in the poorest socio-economic circumstances reached educational levels that were substantially higher than those reached by white pupils in the same circumstances: 33 per cent, as mentioned above, compared with only 22 per cent of white pupils.

☐ Pakistani heritage pupils not affected by poverty had lower levels of attainment than white pupils in the same circumstances: 46 per cent compared with 55 per cent.

The second of these bullet points is particularly interesting. Further research is needed to establish its meaning. It might suggest that there is considerable

LIFE CHANGES

Box 11

For richer, for poorer
– five social class categories in modern Britain, 2003

Wealthy achievers
Represent 25 per cent of the population. Tend to live in a detached house with four or more bedrooms, with more than one car on the drive. Work in managerial or professional occupations. Aged between 45 and 65 but there is a mix of families with children, empty nesters and the retired. Combined income over £50,000, own unit trusts, stocks and shares, and have private health insurance. Like golf and wine. Spend more than £250 a month on credit cards.

Urban prosperous
Represent 11 per cent of the population. Live in multicultural area close to a university. Between 25 and 35 years old with a degree and often single. Interests include theatre and the arts, skiing, herbal/health foods, foreign travel and current affairs. Well-paid executive jobs combine with a lack of mortgage and family commitments. They use the internet for financial affairs.

Comfortably off
Represent 27 per cent of the population. Middle income owner-occupiers with mortgage on a semi-detached house. Children still at home and foreign holidays taken once a year. They try to pay off credit card bills but are not always successful.

Moderate means
Represent 15 per cent of the population. Live in traditional blue-collar terraces. Work in a shop or factory, and less likely to have savings, ISAs or unit trusts. Take fewer holidays than average, have a low credit card limit and spend carefully. Not into the internet, but might have cable TV.

Hard pressed
Represent 22 per cent of the population. Live in overcrowded – typically high-rise or purpose-built – flats and property rented from local council or housing association. Travel to work by bus, tube or on foot and often need a loan to tide them through. Tight budget encourages catalogue shopping to spread payments over time. Recreation: angling or gambling on horses or at the bingo hall. Preponderance of single-parent families.

Source: CACI market research, published autumn 2003

---

resilience in low-income Pakistani heritage families and households and that, compared with the majority community, they are coping remarkably well with the material disadvantage in which they find themselves. The resilience is all the more remarkable in view of the type of anti-Muslim and anti-Kashmiri hostility and criticism that is illustrated in box 12. The source of the resilience almost certainly includes high parental expectations and high levels of parental support and encouragement.

Implications
From the brief discussion above of research findings relating to ethnicity and social class it follows that measures to raise the attainment of Pakistani heritage pupils need to be of three kinds:

☐ those which are **precisely the same** as for raising the attainment of all pupils in the same economic circumstances, for example the measures in programmes such as Education Action Zones, Excellence in Cities, the Schools Facing Challenging Circumstances programme, SureStart, and local schemes supported by the Single Regeneration Budget or European funding

WORK IN PROGRESS • 27

☐ those which in most respects are the same as for all pupils in the same circumstances, but are **not difference-blind**, for example not blind to the fact that the Islamic faith is a significant component in the identity of most British Pakistanis, and not blind to the realities of racism and Islamophobia.

☐ those which are **distinctively and centrally responsive** to British Pakistani experience and concerns in British society.

In the next main section of this book there are several case study examples of the second and third types of measure: (a) measures that are not culture-blind and (b) measures that are responsive to British Pakistani experience and concerns. Such measures will presumably be denounced by the editor who wrote the leader quoted in Box 12. However, the case studies both illustrate and strengthen the arguments for them.

Box 12

Hampering the process of assimilation?
– a view of root causes

The city's Muslim Mirpuri population has not integrated. By pandering to the cultural, linguistic and religious needs of this often fractious community, the education authority has only succeeded in hampering the process of assimilation. Furthermore, by portraying schools and teachers as institutionally racist – an idea reinforced by the Macpherson report into the death of Stephen Lawrence – the authorities have created the impression that the root cause of under-achievement among Muslims is racism in the wider society and not the shortcomings in the habits, customs and behaviour of the immigrant population.

Editorial, Yorkshire Post, *25 July 2003*

4 WHAT'S GOING ON?
– the interpretation of data and trends

SUMMARY

A local education authority has higher standards amongst its Pakistani heritage learners than many other authorities. But recently the GCSE results for such learners were disappointingly poor. The chapter considers the possible reasons for this and quotes the views of a range of Pakistani heritage professionals. A recurring emphasis amongst the professionals was that the expectations of teachers in mainstream schools are too low. The chapter is based on a paper by Nicola Davies, an educational consultant who was until recently a teacher in Slough.

The story

In 1998, just 32 per cent of Pakistani and Kashmiri heritage pupils in Slough gained five or more A*- C GCSE passes, almost 11 percentage points below the LEA average, which was itself below the national average. Similarly only 52 per cent of Pakistani heritage 11 year olds achieved a Level 4 or above in English and 43 per cent in maths compared with LEA averages of 65 and 53 per cent, thirteen and ten percentage points below the LEA averages. Only 28 per cent of Pakistani secondary students were in selective schools compared with 43 per cent of all LEA students.

By 2001 there appeared to be much to celebrate. Results were rising overall and results for Pakistani and Kashmiri heritage pupils were rising faster than national averages and faster than the results of pupils of other backgrounds. Differentials in attainment had been reduced to single figures at the end of both primary and secondary education. Forty-five per cent of Pakistani heritage pupils gained five or more A*- C GCSE passes, only nine percentage points below the LEA average. Similarly 70 per cent of Pakistani heritage 11 year olds achieved a Level 4 or above in English and 63 per cent in maths, now only four and nine percentage points below the LEA average. At this point it seemed that LEA policies were leading to a significant reduction in inequalities of outcome in local schools.

But over the next two years the gap widened once more. In summer 2002, at the end of both primary and secondary education the test results of Pakistani and Kashmiri heritage pupils fell quite significantly. Only 42 per cent of Pakistani heritage pupils gained five or more A*- C GCSE passes. Only 62 per cent achieved a Level 4 or above in English and maths at KS2. Differentials in attainment between Pakistani and Kashmiri heritage pupils and the LEA and white pupil averages were creeping back into double figures. Significantly, no change could be detected in the proportion of Pakistani and Kashmiri pupils entering selective schools.

What happened? What contributed to the rise in achievement? What caused the later decline? These questions are explored here. The chapter does not come up with definitive answers. It does, however, show the broad hypotheses that need to be posited, the detailed questions that have to be asked and the difficult debates and issues that have to be faced. The chapter is informed by semi-structured interviews with Pakistani and Kashmiri heritage teachers, educational support staff, community educationalists and advisers. They discussed successes and pitfalls, and what they consider to be a respectful and high quality education for their children.[1]

The context

Slough is a medium sized, multi-ethnic, multi-faith town on the outskirts of Greater London. According to its 2000 Ofsted inspection report:

> Its most notable characteristic is the multi-skilled, ethnically and socially diverse population that has a wide range of expectations and aspirations for education. Economic factors indicate that the extensive business community makes Slough a relatively prosperous borough, but many Slough residents work outside the town in low-paid employment. Seventy per cent of those employed in Slough are not local residents. Other social measures related to poor housing conditions, low levels of adult education and below average earnings confirm that sections of the town's population have considerable needs.

The town has a long and continuing history of migration and settlement. Of the 119,067 residents, 37 per cent identified themselves in the 2001 census as not-white. Twelve per cent of the total population are of Pakistani heritage. In Slough as in most other areas of Britain the age profile of Pakistani heritage people is different from that of the white population. The make-up of the school population, in consequence, is significantly different from that of the town as a whole. More than a half (54 per cent) of pupils are not white. Just over a fifth of all pupils in the town's schools (21 per cent) are of Pakistani or Kashmiri heritage.

The uses of data

There is a debate in Slough, as elsewhere in Britain, about the usefulness of publishing and studying statistics which cross-tabulate educational achievement with ethnicity. One view is that the focus should be on improving educational achievement for all pupils and that this will be sufficient to raise the achievement of Pakistani and Kashmiri pupils. To focus on just one community, according to this view, is divisive and could create community tensions. This colour-blind approach – more accurately, it is difference-blind – is considered by critics to have been the dominant approach amongst the town's senior administrators when Slough became a unitary authority in 1997. In due course, however, the LEA took a number of explicit and focused measures to reduce inequalities in educational achievement, as outlined later in this chapter.

Box 13

English must come first, says vicar
– a glimpse of a climate of opinion

Community leaders must ensure Asian youngsters are fluent in English or watch them continue to fail at school, a leading churchman has warned... [He] said he was not surprised by research which revealed children, especially in the Pakistani community, were under-achieving in school ... Efforts to improve standards at school had to be supported in the home and community...'I can imagine a poor child sitting in a classroom listening carefully to the lesson but only understanding half of what has been said. Parents from ethnic minorities will naturally want their children to learn their mother tongue. But at the same time they must learn English. Muslim parents will, of course, send their children to the mosque to learn Arabic so that they can recite the Koran. But at the same time they must learn English'.

Source: Slough Observer *15 January 1999*

An entirely different kind of reason for reluctance to publish and publicise data is to do with the policies and practices that may then ensue. All too often, a heavy emphasis on data can lead to target-setting that is narrowly concerned with improving the grades of a smallish number of pupils in order to raise a school's position in league tables, and to streaming and grouping pupils according to their perceived potential. Studies in Britain and in a range of other countries have shown that when an education system places great emphasis on grades and streaming there is little or no benefit for pupils who are already disadvantaged.[2]

A third reason for caution about the use of statistics is the severe danger of reinforcing negative stereotypes and self-fulfilling prophecies. 'No wonder the results at our school are so poor,' a white teacher was heard to say after being briefed about statistics on achievement and ethnicity. 'Our problem is, too many of our children are Pakistanis.' Negative views of the

Box 14

Some of the children are a real worry – a further glimpse of a climate of opinion

...The librarian, who has worked at the comprehensive school for two years, said: 'About 95 per cent of the 560 pupils are of Muslin origin. Most originate from three villages in the disputed Mirpur region of Kashmir on India's border with Pakistan. Large numbers have settled in the school's catchment area. It is like a parallel universe. They have created a Kashmiri ghetto, and the children are not allowed to adopt any western values or customs. Some of the children are a real worry. We have pupils who will come up to you and smile sweetly and say something in Urdu. Later you discover that they have called you a bitch. But most of them are decent kids and so are their families.

Yet whereas Indian children are encouraged at school, the Pakistanis are not. They watch only Pakistani programmes on cable or satellite. Their mothers never learn to speak English. The girls are treated as second class and all are sent home to marry their first cousins in pre-arranged weddings. They receive no support in their studies. If we interfere we are called racists. Yet they hate Sikhs with a vengeance, they hate Hindus and Afro-Caribbeans, and they don't much like us either. They will go Sikh-bashing at the weekend. When I have offered advice to a Muslim girl who came to me and said, 'Please miss, I don't want to get married', I am not supposed to offer her any help. I am not meant to say, 'You are in Britain. This is a free country. You don't have to do anything against your will.'

The librarian said that although parents actively resisted any assimilation – packing children off to Kashmir if they showed signs of becoming westernised – she did not believe that the scenes she witnessed in the classroom were inspired in the home. 'Most are not sophisticated enough for that. Other forces are at work, maybe through their Muslim youth leaders and out on the streets. We recently had Islamic literature circulating that was deeply offensive. Islam is being peddled to these kids. They are told to hate the West, and America in particular. These children are victims, growing up in a country they are forbidden to become a part of and encouraged to despise the people they live amongst'.

Source: Daily Telegraph *13 September 2001*

Pakistani and Kashmiri communities may also be expressed through the local media, as shown in Box 13.

The negative views expressed in Box 13 are mild compared with those of a librarian in a Slough school which were given prominence in the national press shortly after 11 September 2001. The Pakistani community in Slough, the librarian said, has 'created a Kashmiri ghetto and the children are not allowed to adopt any western values or customs ... Their mothers never learn to speak English. The girls are treated as second class and all are sent home to marry their first cousins in pre-arranged weddings. They receive no support in their studies. If we interfere we are called racists...' There is a fuller quotation in box 14. It shows in vivid detail the hostility, fear and ignorance with which anyone wanting to work on improving the life-chances of British Pakistani learners has to deal.

Statistical evidence of low teacher expectations of Pakistani heritage pupils was inadvertently provided in the late 1990s when Slough published data on schools'

predictions of their pupils' later achievements. The predictions for pupils of Pakistani and Kashmiri heritage were significantly less challenging and, it turned out, less accurate than for pupils of other backgrounds.

Action by the LEA

To address the context of fact and opinion outlined above, and despite the acknowledged dangers, the LEA placed great emphasis, in the first instance, on supporting schools with effective data analysis and target setting by ethnicity. This won praise from Ofsted, as shown in Box 15.

Academic English

It was recognised that there are key issues for young Pakistani heritage people around bilingual support and the acquisition of academic English. In consequence the LEA adopted an Australian EAL training course for serving teachers which concentrated on helping

> **Box 15**
>
> ## Highly regarded service
> ### – praise for a local authority
>
> The LEA provides a highly regarded service to its schools. The provision of a comprehensive range of data with a detailed LEA analysis is a strength of the LEA. All schools receive a helpful analysis of their performance data. This includes comparisons with other schools in Slough and draws upon pupil-level data and value-added data. Pupil performance is analysed fully by gender and according to the ethnic heritage of pupils. For secondary schools, it is also analysed according to the type of school... Schools make good use of these data, which received high praise in every school visited during the inspection. They use the data to target teaching resources, to identify pupils in need of support and to evaluate the effectiveness of their strategies to raise standards.
>
> *Source: Ofsted report on Slough, 2001*

learners of EAL to become fluent users of academic English.[3] Attendance on the training course was strongly supported for all mainstream teachers within the education action zone (EAZ) which included all the schools where Pakistani and Kashmiri pupils formed the majority population.

An independent research evaluation commissioned by the authority of the Australian EAL training programme found that a key issue emerging from the teacher discourse following the training was that participants felt they had become particularly attuned to cultural awareness issues which helped them communicate much better with the pupils. In addition, the LEA invested in improving the outcomes of community language teaching in schools and complementary schools through the appointment of a specialist teacher to organise training, grant allocation and support for schools.

The development of specific action projects and partnerships began in earnest after the devolution of EMAG funding schools in 1999. A secondary school project that was typical of many involved tackling the underachievement of girls of Pakistani heritage in science. Lesson plans were developed which emphasised techniques and activities supportive of

more advanced EAL learners. Pakistani students' attitudes to science were sampled and when it emerged that they had had little contact with adults from the Pakistani community involved in the wide range of science-related occupations, an event was organised where Pakistani adults involved in the science field addressed students and parents. A video was also made illustrating the contribution of Black women to Science.

Evaluation of such school-based projects showed that they could have a significant impact on achievement, but only when a number of favourable conditions were met. These included: support from the educational hierarchy, a commitment to combating racism, and well qualified and supported bilingual EMA staff.

What went wrong?

Despite the positive projects and developments outlined above, the GCSE results of Pakistani heritage students in 2002 showed a marked decline when compared with the gradual improvements that had taken place in the previous years. Why? A researcher investigated this question by interviewing a number of Pakistani heritage professionals who knew the local school system well. Comments from the interviews are quoted in Box 16.

Reflections

What can be learned from this sometimes painful journey in one authority towards a fuller understanding of the issues relating to the achievement of Pakistani and Azad Kashmiri pupils? From study of the story and analysis of the interviews a number of tentative observations can be drawn that may help to develop and sustain good practice. Box 17 reports the reflections of the researcher who wrote the paper on which this chapter has been based.

Box 16

What went wrong? – views and opinions concerning under-achievement

I know that there are some really passionate, caring, good teachers, excellent teachers. And some of those excellent teachers turn some of our youngsters around. I know that. So I don't want to just dismiss every teacher in all our schools or every headteacher. I just feel they are too insular, they're not open to the community. The community don't know what's going on in the school, they just think the school knows best and if they send their kids, they will get an education. But they don't know what's going on inside. Schools need to have a real partnership with the community sector, real partnerships with the faith groups and with the parents. (*Community adviser*)

I think there are attitudinal issues that affect achievement, relating to attitude of teachers and the whole establishment and I think that underpins a lot of what's happening in schools...I'd go so far as saying there's, there are teachers in schools that teach children who have no belief in their abilities. (*Advisory teacher*)

I'ts just 'This is a Muslim, he prays five times a day and he fasts one month a year and he goes on Haj.' And that's it. That's not being a Muslim, there's a lot more to being a Muslim. And it's not even just about how a Muslim practises his faith but it's actually the contribution that Islam has made that needs to be included. (*Community adviser*)

There's very little recruitment or positive action towards recruitment of teachers from black and minority ethnic communities. Certainly you have a lot of teaching assistants, but there's a whole range of issues around them, it's actually very difficult for them to develop and move up within organisations. There's a lot of bullying and harassment. (*Family social worker*)

Parents do actually have concern that their children are not achieving as well as the English children, or children from other countries as well. .. [But] when the parents come, they can't push the establishment and the teachers, as they can't speak English. And they don't come forward to speak to teachers, the headteachers or anybody because they feel very uptight. Because they can't explain the situation, they can't explain the concern.

English people, whenever they have any concern, they know what to say, what to ask, they come... But these parents, they don't come, because they just think 'our children are OK. We can't ask for more'. They don't know how to ask for more. (*Teacher*)

Islamophobia is affecting a lot of people and it's affecting a lot of educated people as well. And generations that are coming are going to be affected by it if it doesn't get dealt with really quickly. (Support assistant)

Pakistani children suffer from being labelled as terrorists and in classrooms where teachers appear to talk about issues such as the war with Iraq but discuss it in such a racist way that pupils get offended. (*Community adviser*)

This new generation of kids are crucial to us now. If we want a harmonious future for Slough we have to invest in them. We are trying our best to make sure the kids that come out of our school are going to be the catalysts, the pebbles in the pond making ripples in Slough of moderation and modernisation. Kids feel and look a lot more frightened. They are very conscious of the fact that they are Muslims. (*Complementary school teacher*).

Overall, the Pakistani community has gone past caring because so much has gone on around the world and there's been so much bad focus on Muslims that they're thinking 'It's just not worth trying to voice your opinions or express your ideas because it's just not going to happen'. They feel like there's just too much bad publicity they're not going to be heard in the first place. (*Support assistant*)

There are a lot of parents who want a good foundation in Islamic values for their children. Since September 11 there has been opposition to Muslim schools, but I am tired of Islam being linked with fundamentalism. Muslim values are about family and looking after your family and your elders. (*Community educationalist*)

Source: interviews conducted by Nicola Davies, summer 2003

Box 17

What can be learnt? – reflections on a story

The context of power relationships

A focus on Pakistani and Kashmiri pupil achievement is only useful if accompanied by an understanding of power relationships and the workings of racist disadvantage. Without this, a focus on the use of performance data to quantify progress and success appears to encourage a cultural pathology which problematises Pakistani and Kashmiri communities. Such a pathology distracts educators from their powerful enabling role with pupils, parents and communities. Education professionals need to be supported to understand that a focus on product rather than process by its very nature discourages a critical examination of power structures and leads to systematic devaluing of 'other' linguistic, cultural, and religious capital.

The need for change

A focus on Pakistani and Kashmiri pupil achievement must be accompanied by a willingness to recognise and accept a need for change. Change can be at an individual level as 'individual educators are never powerless, although they frequently work in conditions that are oppressive both for them and their students. While they rarely have complete freedom, educators do have choices in the way they structure the micro-interactions in the classroom' (Cummins, 1996). There are numerous examples of ways in which renegotiations of power can happen, through positive interactions at micro level, within classrooms, between parents, pupils and educators, changing the perceptions of students, colleagues and communities through classroom practice.

'Turning up the volume' of Pakistani and Kashmiri voices within education was welcomed by the whole educational community and the efficacy of individual change can help defeat the 'discourse of despair'.

But a more powerful change in the life chances of Pakistani and Kashmiri pupils will not be effected without a willingness for structures to change.

Successful educational initiatives designed to promote achievement can only be formed with the full participation of pupils and communities themselves in a genuine partnership. This will involve in some senses a change in the power relationships between professionals, pupils, parents and communities and a re-evaluation of the relationship between the 'doers' and the 'done to', between 'us' and 'them'.

Who decides?

Institutions need to respond to demands for a respectful and high quality education for Pakistani and Kashmiri young people. The key question is who decides on the learning that we value and want to happen? For most parents, including most Muslim parents, education is more that just schooling and education needs to encompass consideration and respect for the 'whole child', including respect for language, culture and faith.

Infrastructure

An LEA should be able to provide the infrastructure which enables innovation and collaboration to flourish at classroom, school and community levels. The conversion of a local school to become an Islamic primary school could be viewed as an opportunity to develop collaborative rather than coercive relations of power, the LEA providing the venue and monitoring the standards and the faith community being enabled to provide a space to support the negotiation of identity for young people.

A better 'us'

Islamophobia endangers the well-being of all communities, and can be detected not just through crude racism but also through the systematic exercise of coercive power. Promoting collaborative power relations creates a better and more meaningful 'us'.

Source: Views, Voices and Visibility: realising the achievement of Muslim pupils of Pakistani and Kashmiri heritage *by Nicola Davies, 2003*

5 MAGIC INGREDIENTS?
– the views and reflections of learners

SUMMARY

Careful monitoring had enabled a local authority to identify that two of its secondary schools were bucking the trend in relation to the achievement of Pakistani-heritage boys. A researcher met with some of the high-achieving students themselves and obtained their own angle on the factors underlying their success. This chapter outlines the questions that were asked and reports on the boys' views. It is based on a paper by Sameena Choudry, until recently teacher adviser in Sheffield and now head of the bilingual support service in North Lincolnshire.

Messages from performance data

Sheffield LEA performance data for 2002 showed that 41 per cent of all students taking the GCSE examinations achieved 5 A*-C grades. Girls in the city outperformed boys by eight percentage points (boys 37 per cent, girls 45), as is the case nationally. Disaggregated data according to both gender and ethnicity showed that only 19 per cent of Pakistani heritage boys gained five A*-C grades. The percentage for Pakistani heritage girls was 26.5.

When the LEA-level data on Pakistani heritage students was compared with school-level data it was clear that two schools were spectacularly bucking the trend. At one, 55 per cent of Pakistani boys gained five A*-C grades. At the other, the proportion was 50 per cent. In the first of these schools the Pakistani girls outperformed the boys (67 per cent compared with 55) but in the second the boys outperformed the girls (50 per cent compared with 38).[1]

What was going on? Did these two schools have a magic ingredient that could be acquired by other schools? This was the question that a researcher investigated. She interviewed members of the senior management teams in both schools and asked them what they thought the secrets of their success might be. Their answers are shown and discussed in chapter 11. Also, she interviewed two groups of Year 11 boys at the schools and distributed a questionnaire. The boys' answers form the basic subject-matter of this chapter.

A shortened version of the interview schedule is shown in box 18. In both schools, much the same range of responses was received. For this reason the responses are discussed below thematically rather than school by school.[2]

High expectations and aspirations

When questioned as to what they felt was the single most important factor in their being academically successful the most frequent answer at the one school was high expectations. The boys were expected to do well and there was pressure from home to succeed. This was closely reinforced by the school at every opportunity (for example at assemblies and in tutor time) and was clearly led by the head and senior management team. Also it was mentioned that older students frequently act as valuable role models, for example in their progression post-16 and in entry to higher education.

Ability to disengage from negative peer group pressure.

Although the boys were influenced by peer group pressure and engaged in minor misbehaviour in lessons at times, they were well aware of the dynamics of what was going on and how it could have a negative impact on their learning. In consequence they had developed strategies to disengage from peer culture and to be focused on their learning.

(continued on page 38)

Box 18

WHAT MAKES THE DIFFERENCE?
STUDENT DISCUSSION GROUPS ON RAISING ATTAINMENT OF PAKISTANI BOYS
GUIDANCE NOTES FOR INTERVIEWER

Introduction

Give a brief overview of the project – that it is a research project looking at what secondary schools have done to improve the performance of students of Pakistani heritage, in particular boys.

Explain to them that I have talked to teachers and now I want to find out what students think about their school and what helps them in their learning.

Tell them I will be asking them general views on their school and about the ways their school helps them to achieve to the best of their ability.

Assure them that nothing they say will be reported to their teachers and that the discussion will be summarised and completely anonymous. Names of individuals will be changed in any quotes used.

Overall views of the school

Do they think it is a good school? What do they base their opinions on – exam results, teachers, facilities? Do they think it is a good school for Pakistani students?

In general, what do they feel about teachers in their school? Are they helpful, is there a climate of praise, are they fair?

Do they think that resources are good in the school? Enough textbooks, computer facilities, buildings and so on? Do Pakistani students have equal access to these resources and do they benefit as much as they could?

What types of extra-curricular activities are available that the students have taken part in? Do they feel that they have helped to improve their learning or exam performance?

Do they think that the public face of the school (displays, brochures and pamphlets, and the use of pupils in positions of public responsibility) gives out clear messages about the value the school places on its Pakistani pupils?

What in their opinion has been the single main factor in the overall success of Pakistani boys at their school?

What other factors may have contributed to their school's success in raising the attainment of Pakistani boys? Leadership and management? Assessment and monitoring, use of data, self-evaluation? Quality of teaching and commitment of staff? Resources, accommodation and facilities? School culture and ethos? Curriculum and extra-curricular activities? External and community links? Whole-school commitment to antiracism and equality of opportunity? Specific targeted work with individuals (for example, mentoring, EAL, mother tongue)? Specific targeted work focusing on gender and attainment? Any other major initiatives the school is involved in, for example Excellence in Cities?

Do they think students of all backgrounds have benefited from increased academic performance at the school? Are there any aspects of the school's current practice that hinders Pakistani-heritage students' performance? In what ways? What strategies are in place to resolve these issues?

Gender and attainment

There are many suggested reasons for boys' underachievement. What do you think are the causes for your achievement?

What are your views on the solutions to underachievement of boys? Do you feel any of these solutions have contributed to your own success?

Do you think there are any additional causes for the underachievement of Pakistani heritage boys that are not included on the list? What do you think the solutions for these particular causes could be? What advice would you give Pakistani pupils, teachers and senior management teams in other secondary schools to raise the attainment of Pakistani students?

Box 18 continued

Look at the widely-held perceptions about gender and achievement on the attached sheet. What do think about these? (*Give out list.*) Are there any that are particularly relevant to Pakistani students?

Attitudes to school

List the attitudinal characteristics which seem to have made you successful learners.

Where do you think you get these attitudinal characteristics from?

Are there additional attitudinal characteristics you need to have to be successful in school if you are a boy from a Pakistani background?

Boys and peer group pressure

Is there a gender difference in attitudes to school work and is there such a thing as peer group pressure that is strongly anti-work? If these exist where do they come from?

Are there particular attitudinal differences (either positive or negative) that can be attributed to Pakistani students in general and boys in particular? Where do you think these come from? What do you think can be done by schools to develop positive attitudes to school work?

The school's influence

List the characteristics of effective teachers and ineffective teachers (for example, doesn't shout, is firm, listens, is fair to all, is friendly, respects class, has high standards, explains things).

Are there particular characteristics of effective teachers that benefit successful learning in Pakistani students in general and boys in particular?

What is the extent and variety of teaching methods used in school? Which do they most enjoy or find most helpful? Do teachers always teach them as a whole class, do they do pair work, work in groups?

What support is available to help students do their best? Are they given help on how to work (study skills), to set themselves targets, (tutorial support, target setting, mentoring)? Do all students receive the support they need?

To what extent do they feel they are expected to take responsibility for their own learning?

Do they prefer coursework or one-off examinations to show what they have learned? Or a mixture? Why? Which is of most benefit to pupils of Pakistani heritage?

Do they think that some subjects are boys' subjects and some are girls' subjects? Are some subjects particularly attractive for pupils of Pakistani heritage to study. If so, why?

Finally

If they had a chance, is there anything they would change about their school to help them improve their learning? What changes would benefit students of Pakistani heritage in general and boys in particular?

What specific advice would you give other secondary schools about raising and sustaining Pakistani boys' examination performance?

Source: adapted slightly from a questionnaire compiled by Sameena Choudry, Sheffield Education Department, 2003. One of the pieces of discussion material she used ('Things people say') is reproduced in box 19.

Footsteps[3]

Researcher	What in your opinion is the most important single factor in you being academically successful?
Zubair	I want a good education
Khalid	Family and friends and that say you should get a good education, 'cos all the time you want to get somewhere. Most Asian people don't do very good jobs, you know like working in takeaways or taxis and so on. They [*referring to family and friends*] don't want me to do that, neither do I, so I work hard.
Nabeel	I want to get a good job and that.
Shahid	My family have high expectations of me and I want to achieve.
Shafiq	Family pressure and support. Also I have an older sister that has done well academically and my family would like me to follow in her footsteps.

They were able to be part of the in-crowd whilst also getting on academically and were successful in not being seen as 'swots' by their peers. Their capacity to navigate between two worlds was an important aspect of their identity and they took quiet pride in it.

The capacity involved taking a long view of their own lives and a sense of their possible and preferred futures. They saw education instrumentally, namely as a means to an end, the end being upward mobility. They were not totally immune from peer group pressure but were alert to the times when adolescent behaviour and norms were in danger of getting out of control and of adversely affecting their chances of gaining academic success.

Box 19

Things people say
– but what do you think?

Why do girls do better at school nowadays than boys?

Girls are cleverer

Adolescence affects boys more adversely than girls

Girls get more attention

Girls are better at coursework

Young boys have fewer good role models at home and in school

Changes in employment patterns have benefited girls more than boys

Boys pay less attention to homework

Equal opportunities legislation has worked against boys

Boys do not read as widely as girls – they fall behind at primary school and never close the gap

Boys are more independent than girls and are more anti-authority.

Source: from discussion material devised by Sameena Choudry, 2003

Effective home school links and outreach.
The schools had effective relationships with the boys' homes and these were seen by the boys as involving a genuine two-way process. They gave examples of teachers undertaking home visits, liaising with community organisations and attending local mosques on a regular basis. They mentioned that in general their parents felt comfortable attending school for any matter and the school would communicate directly with parents when necessary.

Race relations throughout the school
At one school, boys stated that when they had initially come to the school in Year 7 there were racial tensions and little mixing between white and minority ethnic pupils. As a result they had been involved in clashes with other students, since they had felt they needed to stand up for themselves. However, now they were in KS4 they felt that relations between students of different backgrounds were much improved. Racist

As if we belong here

Shayek	There's Mr A, he teaches science and do you know miss [referring to me] he's also a Hafiz [Muslim religious scholar]...
Kashif she	Yes, and there is also Miss I, also teaches science. We also have Mr M, he teaches maths and there are also other Asian teachers in the school such as Mrs A and Mr M and Mr... *(they continue to list the minority ethnic teachers in the school.)*
Shayek	Oh and there is also Mr S, he supports us in ICT.
Researcher	Well, that's quite a few teachers you've mentioned to me. You told me that they made a difference to you? How?
Kashif	Well, they make us feel as if we belong here.

incidents still occurred from time to time but the boys were confident that senior staff dealt with them swiftly, sensitively and effectively. To a certain extent the boys considered that they themselves had to be at the forefront of improving relationships for pupils now coming into the school and they accepted this responsibility.

On the questionnaires they filled in, all but one of the boys stated that other pupils never bullied them and that they never felt unsafe in the playground.

Positive minority ethnic role models in the school at all levels from senior management to technical support

The boys mentioned teachers and support staff as having a positive impact on their wish to succeed academically. They were able to name all the minority ethnic staff and cited their presence in school as making a significant difference to them as students.

The boys were clear and comfortable with the fact that minority ethnic students were an integral part of the school and that their needs were taken into

Everyone is different

Pupils here come from a wide range of ethnic and social backgrounds. That was one of the reasons my parents wanted me to come here. What this means is that there are very few situations where you are seen as being the one who is different. Everyone is different and we as pupils are used to socialising with one another, it's the norm... If there was a racial incident I wouldn't have any problems telling my teachers and I would have full confidence in the matter being investigated properly and dealt with if necessary.

consideration. In both schools the wide social, ethnic and religious mix was seen as a positive asset.

Personal, cultural and religious identity

The boys felt that their school not only built on its academic reputation and gave clear messages of the importance and emphasis on attainment but also balanced this by nurturing the 'whole child'. Their pastoral needs were well taken care of and extra-curricular activities enabled them to develop their personal areas of interest. They considered that students of Pakistani heritage benefited from this as much as everyone else. They cited activities such as the Millennium Volunteers group and the Duke of Edinburgh Awards as examples.

The boys also felt positive that their linguistic and religious needs were taken into consideration. One school teaches Urdu at GCSE and all but one of the boys interviewed had taken advantage of this and gained a qualification. In addition, the schools had made provision for religious needs. For example, there was a room at the other school where students could perform prayers and read the Qur'an. Students were

Just enough

I wish teachers knew a little about my background so that they have a better understanding of my religious and cultural beliefs. Not necessary too much in depth. Just enough to know something about me.

The opportunity to be Muslims

Researcher	What in your opinion has been the main single factor in your overall success?
Shahzaman	My Muslim identity.
Researcher	Can you elaborate? How has this contributed to your academic success?
Shahzaman	Well, Islam teaches you to be self-disciplined in the conduct of your everyday life... For example praying five times every day... you do this at a set time. Next month as you know we will be fasting. It's a way of life. This all makes you very disciplined, you don't really have time to waste when you live your life according to Islamic belief... In addition, Islam really places a high value on the pursuit of knowledge, which I wholeheartedly believe in and that's why I work hard at my studies. At this school there are many students from different ethnic backgrounds who are Muslims and share this goal... We are given the opportunity to be Muslims... See that room over there miss – well, we have copies of the Qur'an Majeed in there for us to read and we can use it to perform prayers if needed. Also we are allowed to go to the local mosque to perform Juma prayers if we want to. The mosque isn't very far from here.

Doing well

Habib	At my other school teachers would help you if you worked hard. If you didn't they weren't really that bothered about how you were doing. I used to get into trouble and not really work but it seemed as if nobody cared. Here, teachers really care and they make sure that you work hard.
Researcher	OK, what about the rest of you, why did you come here?
Khurshid	Whilst I was at primary my mother started looking at which secondary school I should go to so she looked at the league table results and decided on here.
Researcher	Why?
Khalid	Well, their results were good and compared with the other secondary schools within the area where I live they were much better, so she chose this school. Also she was concerned that a lot of the other Pakistani boys in the area where I live didn't bother about school and hung around together in the evenings getting up to no good and she didn't want that for me. So you see she found out information about different schools and then decided what would be the best for me.
Researcher	Do you think she made a good choice?
Khalid	Yes, I like it here and I am doing well.

trusted to attend the local mosque for prayers and during Ramadan consideration was given to those who were fasting.

The boys felt that freedom to express their Muslim identity in school in a positive way was of paramount importance in enabling them to be academically successful. Their Muslim identity transcended their Pakistani heritage identity and created bonds with students of other ethnic groups.

At one school all the boys spoken to lived outside the catchment area in one of the three least prosperous areas of the city where there was an established Pakistani heritage community. They mentioned that their parents had chosen to send them to this particular school because of its league table results and positive reputation within the community itself. In many cases elder siblings had also attended the school and this had given them advantage in gaining a place at the school, which is heavily subscribed. All felt that the school had lived up to their parents' high expectations.

Concluding notes

In addition to interviewing students at two schools about the factors underlying their success, the researcher interviewed senior staff. Their responses are reported in chapter 11 within the context of discussions of school management and leadership. There was substantial agreement between the two sets of interviews. Both referred to the importance of high expectations, of combining pastoral and academic approaches in a concern for 'the whole child', of recognising and respecting British Muslim identity, and of maintaining good relationships between homes and school. Home-school cooperation is the subject of the next chapter.

As this chapter draws to its close, it is relevant to note that the focus group discussions reported here almost certainly had a valuable impact on the boys themselves. For they were given space not only to talk and articulate but also to reflect. It was almost certainly beneficial for them to consider their own learning, development and education. There are many other examples in this book of children and young people being given space to talk and reflect. One of the purposes of the book is to encourage such conversations between the young and adults, and between lay people and professionals.

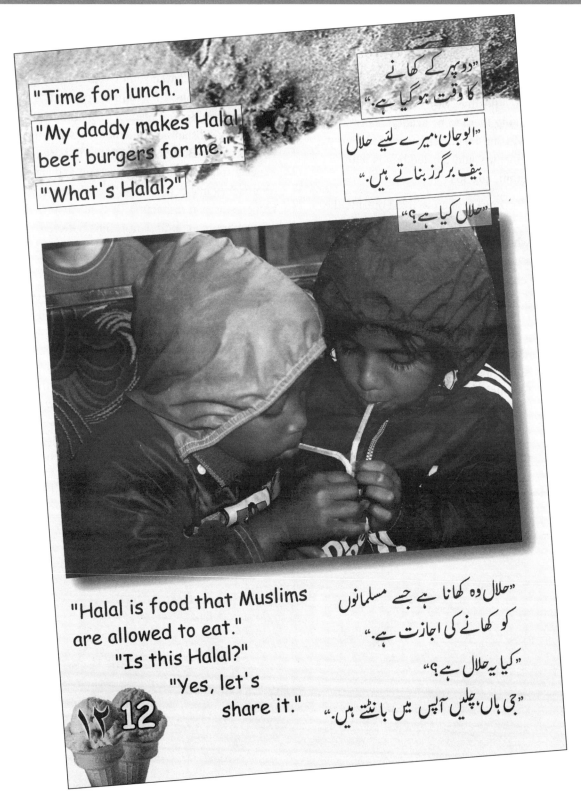

Stimulating and supporting bilingualism, rightly understood, promotes achievement in a range of ways. Several organisations and companies have responded to the need for good quality dual-language books. The example on this page includes cultural content and is copied from Are We There Yet? *published in 2003 by Primary Colours, Huddersfield.*

Bilingual books featuring pupils help to foster links between home and school. Such links are the subject matter of the next chapter.

6 NOT JUST WRITING LETTERS

consulting and working with parents

SUMMARY

There is substantial research evidence that the achievement of children and young people in school is related to the kinds of relationship that schools build and maintain with parents. This chapter describes projects to improve relationships with Pakistani heritage families in Kirklees, Nottingham and Redbridge. It draws on reports by Jo Pilling and Shazia Azhar, who are members of the EMA service in Kirklees; Stuart Scott, working as a consultant in Nottingham; and Jannis Abley and Samina Jaffar, members of the EMA service in Redbridge.

A survey

A primary school in Kirklees decided it needed more accurate information about the community that the school served and that in seeking the information it should disregard many or most of the assumptions that staff already had. Specifically, it wanted to know:

☐ the level of education of the adults in each family

☐ the language(s) used for daily communication amongst family members

☐ the language(s) used in written communication within the community

☐ the aspirations of parents for their children.

This single-form entry school is made up of 196 pupils, of whom 125 are of Pakistani or Kashmiri heritage; there are 71 who are white, two of Indian heritage and two Libyans. In total, 109 families filled in and returned the questionnaire described below.

Following consultation with the headteacher and an LEA adviser, the school-based ethnic minority achievement (EMA) co-ordinator produced a draft questionnaire. It was trialled with a small number of parents who were asked not only to complete it but also to talk about their reactions and how they felt about them. The questionnaire was then redrafted, with some of the questions rephrased and others removed altogether, because parents felt that they were intrusive or that their purpose was obscure.

This procedure was repeated until it was considered that the school had a questionnaire that was sensitive to parents as well as addressing the original aims of the project. In addition it was, of course, essential that its format should make it easy to collate the eventual responses

The project began with an announcement at a whole-school assembly in which the headteacher outlined the purpose of the questionnaire and how the resulting information would be used. The children were encouraged to share this information with their families and were told that every family would be receiving a letter and a telephone call about the questionnaire in due course. To make these high priority telephone calls a bilingual classroom support assistant was released from classroom and other duties.

The school recognised the possibility that some of the parents might have difficulty in completing the questionnaire in writing and that there would be greater consistency in responses if parents were provided with some support. The support took the form of informal meetings between teaching staff and parents, facilitated by bilingual members of staff when needed. The EMA coordinator was a speaker of Punjabi and Urdu and two curriculum support workers who identified themselves as Pahari speakers participated actively. There is currently much debate regarding the status of Pahari and whether it is a language in its own right or a variant of Punjabi. The debate is inevitably influenced by the current political

climate in the region of Kashmir. The school chose to refer to Pahari in order to show respect for the parents' perceptions and definitions.

Four meetings relating to the questionnaire were arranged at various times over two days. Each began with an explanation of national and local underachievement of Pakistani and Kashmiri heritage pupils when compared with LEA and national attainment levels at Key Stages 1 and 2. The questionnaire was presented as a way forward for the community the school served. Parents' responses to it would help identify specific issues or potential barriers to learning that staff and parents could address in partnership together. Parents were then invited to complete the questionnaire with staff available to offer clarification and answer any specific queries.

Parents found most of the questions easy to answer. Questions about language and languages, however, proved problematic. Some parents could not in the first instance name the language they used in everyday life with precision – they simply called it 'Pakistani'. They were helped to identify their language with confidence, however, as either Punjabi or Pahari, through discussion with bilingual staff. Such discussion was much welcomed. Being able to identify their language positively and having the terminology to label it appropriately enhanced their self-confidence and sense of personal identity. Subsequently Pahari speaking parents identified themselves on school forms as Pahari rather than Punjabi speakers.

The principal findings are summarised in box 20.

Follow-up
As a result of the findings summarised in box 20, the following actions were taken:

☐ An initial meeting was held where parents could discuss the conclusions drawn from the questionnaire

☐ The school suggested a programme of action to take place over the following year to address the issues they had identified, and invited parents to comment and suggest further actions the school might take

---

Box 20

Backgrounds and hopes
Results from a survey of parents

Aspirations
All parents stated that they wanted their children to exceed their own achievements. By and large, however, it was only those who had personal experience of higher or further education who saw this as an aspiration for their children.

Higher education
Considerably more parents had had higher education, mainly in Pakistan, than the school had predicted.

Experience of the English education system
Amongst the Punjabi and Pahari speaking families there were some in which one parent had no personal experience of the English education system. It was only in the Pahari speaking group that there were families in which neither parent had such experience.

Knowledge of education
Parents felt that they lacked knowledge about their children's education and in consequence were not confident in approaching the school or individual teachers; they definitely had a strong desire for their children to experience academic success but were unsure of their own role in helping to ensure this.

Self-definition
Of the families previously recorded by the school as Pakistani, many identified themselves as Kashmiri.

Naming of home language
Prior to the questionnaire the school had recorded the heritage language of all Pakistani pupils as either Punjabi or Urdu; subsequently several families identified themselves as Pahari speakers.

Trepidation
In conversation, several parents said they felt trepidation when needing or wishing to make contact with the school.

- [ ] A timetable of discussion meetings was drawn up to raise parental awareness of systems to plot pupil progress and what this means for their child

- [ ] Advice and support were offered on behaviour management, specifically linked to the school's own policy and practice

- [ ] Literacy and numeracy workshops were organised to inform parents about current teaching and learning styles used nationally and in the school

- [ ] Subsequent meetings provided parents with strategies to support their child at home, including support through heritage language

- [ ] Parents were also given advice on how to support their child with homework

- [ ] Greater emphasis was placed on parent-school liaison in the school improvement plan

- [ ] An oral history project involved parents and grandparents. Every class in the school, on one particular day, received a visit from at least one adult and interviewed her. Many children also interviewed their mothers and grandmothers at home.

Reflections

Although drafting and trialling the questionnaire was time-consuming, staff felt consultation was necessary to arrive at a document that was sensitive to parental feelings whilst obtaining the necessary information. This also ensured maximum participation. The level of responses was extremely high compared with national average questionnaire returns. It was largely due to the support, including bilingual support, offered to parents enabling them to complete the questionnaire in a non-judgemental environment. The high return and the consistent way in which the parents had interpreted and understood the questions rewarded this expenditure of both time and effort.

In a written report on the project the following recommendations were offered for any school wishing to embark on something similar:

- [ ] know from the onset what you want to investigate, and why and how you will use the information you obtain

- [ ] be open minded about the results

- [ ] ensure full support of the senior management team, from the headteacher down

- [ ] fully understand the considerable time commitment.

- [ ] give the questionnaire high profile and status

- [ ] ensure appropriate bilingual support – this could come from informed parents as well as staff, and possibly staff could be 'loaned' from another school

- [ ] use a variety of strategies to reassure parents regarding the purpose and use of the questionnaire information

- [ ] ensure one-to-one contact so that there can be discussion of the questions (before/after school, lunchtimes, any time convenient for parents – be flexible!)

- [ ] provide feedback, both orally and in writing, and both informally and formally, about your findings and proposed actions

- [ ] make sure there are visible and positive outcomes.

Towards shared understandings

Forest Fields Primary School in Nottingham similarly wished to improve relationships and communication with its Pakistani heritage families. After discussion with an outside consultant and with the school's EMA coordinator, it decided to produce a series of booklets about school life that pupils could discuss with their parents. The project is outlined in box 21.

Climates of opinion

Two primary schools in the London Borough of Redbridge resolved to improve their contacts and relationships with Pakistani heritage parents. They began by requesting a member of the LEA's EMA service to talk informally with parents in the playground in order to get a sense of the climate of opinion and to sound out their views on local projects such as Sure Start. It was clear from these initial soundings that there was much mutual misunderstanding. Parents were keen to support their children but did not feel welcomed by the schools. The schools, for their part, were disappointed that

Box 21

Not just writing letters home
The closer involvement of parents

Aims and hopes

Forest Fields Primary School in Nottingham wanted to improve communication with parents and the local community. It was not just a matter of writing better letters home or providing more information in mother tongue. They wanted everyone to have as much information about their children's work as if they had visited the school frequently and had spent time in classrooms as flies on the wall.

Further, they wanted to devise a way of making their practice explicit. They hoped that by doing this they would eliminate parents' mistrust or misunderstandings about what went on in the school. And they wanted to provide something that would improve communication between parents and children about school – they hoped that parents would have useful and exciting discussions with their children about what they did in school. They hoped that as parents and prospective parents understood more about the work of the school, they would feel more confident about visiting and maybe getting more involved in parent support groups.

For instance, they wanted to make more explicit the value of play in the development of language and learning. They hoped parents would understand that apparently random activities were carefully structured and designed to develop scientific enquiry and social skills, and to make sense of the adult world.

Looking around

The headteacher and EMAG coordinator met first to decide how they could best make the work of the school explicit. They looked at booklets produced by other schools and LEAs and particularly liked the photo books with short captions (often with versions in home language), which tried to give glimpses of the school day. They found the books produced by Margaret McMillan Nursery School in Islington and the Service for English as an Additional Language in Brighton and Hove particularly inspiring. They made contact with an ICT team at Nottingham University who agreed to help them to produce a CD-Rom along similar lines. The advantage of this format was that it could include small video clips of classroom events and could give to parents items to listen to as well as read.

Since a CD-Rom would take some time to produce and would only be accessible to parents who had their own computers or could use them through libraries or the school, it was decided to work first on producing picture books. Books, since they would be unique and handmade, could be designed in a variety of ways, including jigsaws, zigzags and large formats. When tried and tested, the books would provide a template for the CD-Rom.

Topics

The following topics were provisionally agreed on:

- [ ] *I Like Reading* would explore the different ways in which children use their reading skills in their first language and English in school, at home and around the city
- [ ] *What did you do in school today?* would show a parent asking the questions and a child providing visual answers
- [ ] *A day in the life of the school* would show all the people who visit, bring things and take things away, from very early till very late
- [ ] *First Day at Nursery School*
- [ ] *Visiting a Farm*
- [ ] Report on an idea going through school council
- [ ] Something on assemblies

The EMAG team worked with classroom teachers to construct frameworks for the books, refine the text and begin collecting appropriate photographs.

Many teachers wanted to involve the children in the production. This would slow the process but meant that parents would find out from their children about the production of the book long before it appeared.

Source: this report is by Stuart Scott, who acted as consultant to the work at Forest Fields Primary School.

approaches they had made to parents had not been successful. Issues requiring joint deliberation included:

- [ ] extended visits abroad

- [ ] the nature and value of play

- [ ] the format of open evenings, social occasions and drop-in sessions

- [ ] the content and style of English classes for adult learners

- [ ] the form of contributions by outside speakers at school assemblies

- [ ] parental support for homework

- [ ] links with local madrasahs.

Not Shakespearean Urdu

A lot of people can read Urdu, but not Shakespearian Urdu, you know. If a letter's difficult, people don't bother reading it. Use everyday English and tell the translators to keep it simple.

– from an interview with a Pakistani-heritage parent, Rotherham, 2003

A practical project

After an examination of the findings, the Pakistani and Muslim Achievement Project (PMAP) was set up. Its intended activities are listed in box 22.

Box 22

Pakistani and Muslim Achievement Project
– plans and priorities in two primary schools

Meet with parents in meetings at school, in the playground and in other organised events to promote the importance of early years education

Work in partnership with Sure Start's educational development officer to provide workshops for parents on the learning gained through different play activities

Promote and re-establish the toy library; offer support on how to use the equipment and encourage parents to obtain construction toys and jigsaws

Work closely with mosque leaders

Organise exchange visits for staff between mainstream schools and madrasahs

Explore possibilities for homework support within the time children spend at the madrasah.

Source: paper by Samina Jaffar and Jannis Abley, Redbridge, 2003

In Pakistan buses are decorated.

Can you decorate this bus?

37

When pupils make extended visits in term-time to the country of their birth or their family's origin, many schools are keen to support their learning whilst they are away and in this way minimise any drop in attainment when the pupil returns to school. Schools also wish to stress that the visit is a valuable learning experience in itself.

To this end, some LEAs have produced high quality material to accompany the visit. The example on this page is copied from Pakistan: Extended Visit Workbook, published by Oldham LEA. It contains various activities and is linked to the National Curriculum, the National Literacy Strategy and the National Numeracy Strategy.

7 BEING A BRITISH MUSLIM
– linking with imams, mosques and madrasahs

SUMMARY

Chapter 7 discusses the vital importance of working in partnership with mosques and madrasahs, and of understanding Islamic concepts of education, knowledge and learning. It describes a partnership between a cluster of schools in Leicester and four madrasahs and refers also to a mentoring scheme in Redbridge involving two local imams. It closes with advice to mainstream schools, LEAs and the complementary sector on practical ways ahead. It is based primarily on a paper by Maurice Irfan Coles, chief executive of the School Development Support Agency, Leicester, and previously senior adviser in Birmingham.

'There is a real need,' writes a British Muslim educationist, 'for teachers and local government officers to understand the Muslim frame of reference, and to use it to help their pupils understand and deal with the issues that preoccupy many British Muslims.' He continues:

> For many Muslims in the UK Islam is the key determinant in their lives. Yet schools are not always sensitive to this. Pupils as they enter through the school portals are required to leave their religion at home, not through design but because so often the school is simply unaware of the centrality of Islam in the life of its Muslim pupils. There is a great and understandable reluctance to begin to debate what it means to be a British Muslim ...

> But such are the forces, pressures and influences on young Muslims that schools must grasp the nettle and engage in open and honest dialogue about what it means to be a British Muslim. The discourse must be one between equals, not one that assumes one set of values is superior to another.[1]

One essential place for such open and honest dialogue is the relationship between madrasahs and mainstream schools. This chapter outlines practical problems and possibilities with descriptions of case studies from Leicester and Redbridge. The principles and assumptions underlying the chapter are set out in box 23.

Madrasahs and mainstream

Moat Community College in Leicester is a mixed comprehensive for the 11-16-age range. It has approximately 1050 students on roll. Ninety-five per cent of its intake is from minority ethnic backgrounds. Roughly 90 per cent are Muslim. The majority of students reside in the Highfields area of Leicester, which is one of the most diverse, densely populated and economically deprived areas in the country. Moat is part of Highfields' small education action zone, known as IMPACT, which comprises one secondary and nine primary schools. Many of the zone's pupils attend supplementary or complementary schools after school and at weekends and, given the Muslim background of the majority, madrasahs predominate.

There is much anecdotal evidence, and some great concern, about the amount of time Muslim children and young people spend at the madrasah. Many schools are seriously worried that after a comparatively long and arduous day in mainstream schools their pupils, boys and girls, and including the very young, break for tea and then go to a madrasah for several hours. Teachers are concerned that the hours spent thus after school have a deleterious effect on work during school time, and consequently on levels of attainment. They are generally aware that their pupils attend after school classes but often have little hard evidence and only the haziest of notions about what attendance at madrasahs involves in practice.

Box 23

To be a British Muslim:
– fifteen propositions

1 Key determinant
Faith and the remembrance of God are key determinants in the lives of many Muslims; an education system that fails to recognise, acknowledge and build upon this is failing its pupils.

2 Revealed and acquired knowledge
Islamic views of learning and of revealed and acquired knowledge are not understood and utilised positively in the mainstream school system.

3 Lack of recognition
The omission of Islamic perspectives and of genuine recognition of Islamic civilisation from the school curriculum serves to undermine the confidence of Muslim pupils, and miseducates non-Muslims by implicitly denying the shared histories and narratives that make up pluralist Britain.

4 Under-attainment
The serious under-attainment of many Muslim pupils, particularly those of Pakistani/ Kashmiri and Bangladeshi heritage requires closer scrutiny and concerted action to close the attainment gap.

5 Debate
A robust, frank and open debate is required about what it means to be a British Muslim. This debate should help British Muslim pupils of both genders in their own attempts to define their identities in Britain in the 21st century.

6 Closer links
Closer links between the mainstream schools, mosques and madrasahs will benefit all Muslim pupils; help raise attainment in the mainstream; and support attempts which schools and madrasahs may wish to make in changing their pedagogic styles.

7 Legislation
The incorporation of an Islamic frame of reference into all policies will support schools and LEAs in fulfilling their statutory requirement under the Race Relations Amendment Act, and help them to demonstrate active implementation of the new positive duty to promote equality.

8 Inspection requirements
Effective responses to meeting the needs of Muslim pupils will satisfy some of the requirements outlined in the new Ofsted framework, especially if schools have proactively involved their pupils.

9 Community cohesion
A strategic approach which is joined up and coherent across the range of national and local government departments will help support the drive for community cohesion and help put an end to the 'parallel lives' and segregation of various communities.

10 World context
The evil and tragic events of 9/11 and its continuing aftermath require attention to the nature of Islam and to the position of Muslims who are citizens of western countries.

11 Islamophobia
The well documented rise of Islamophobia provides an even greater urgency to address these issues.

12 Fundamentalism
The rise of Islamic fundamentalism and sectarianism must be addressed openly so that all sectors of society, Muslims and non-Muslims, can challenge them.

13 Geo-political factors
For Muslim communities, known collectively as the ummah, major geo-political issues such as the Israel-Palestine conflict, the disputes in Kashmir, the religious strife in Gujarat and the presence of non-Muslim armies in Iraq and Afghanistan, are very real and exist here and now; they affect not only the Muslim population but also groups such as British born Jews, those of Hindu Gujarati origin and those of Punjabi Sikh heritage.

14 Double impact
Many people seeking asylum are of Muslim origin and can suffer the double impact of being despised for seeking asylum and for being Muslim.

15 The need for policy
The combination of all the factors listed above has the potential to be the explosive spark that could undermine the roots of our shared multi-faith, multicultural, multi-ethnic, pluralist democracy. The very complexity necessitates a well thought out, clearly articulated strategy at school, LEA and national levels.

Source: Education and Islam: a new strategic approach, *by Maurice Irfan Coles, School Development Support Agency, Leicester, 2004*

For several years now Moat has conducted a homework survey for all pupils. This consists of thirteen questions related to homework habits, for example where, when and for how long homework is undertaken by both genders in each year group. In addition, questions are asked about other commitments, since these are likely to take up time that might be devoted to homework. In this context there are questions about the length of time and frequency of visits to the mosque.

The results are startling. For example, the most recent survey found that 94 per cent of Year 7 boys attended the mosque. Eighty-four per cent went every day throughout the working week and the majority remained there for at least two hours. Although boys' mosque attendance diminishes as they progress through the school, especially in Year 11, there are still a number who are spending considerable amounts of time on mosque activities. The pattern of attendance is

---

Box 24

The nature and value of complementary education
– an interview schedule for visits to madrasahs

General

1 What is the name of the madrasah? What does it mean in English?

2 What are the number, gender, age and ethnicity of your pupils?

3 What areas and schools do your pupils come from?

4 How many classes do you have? What are the pupils' ages?

5 How many teachers/support staff do you have?

6 What are the qualifications of the staff: qualified in UK, or abroad or unqualified

7 How long have your teachers been teaching?

   they have 0 – 5 years experience

   they have 6 – 10 years experience

   they have over 10 years experience

8 What training do you offer to the staff?

9 How is your madrasah organised and run?

10 How is the madrasah funded?

Curriculum and assessment

11 What languages do you teach in?

12 What subjects do you teach?

13 What is your syllabus based on?

   external syllabus (which)

   internal syllabus

   neither (please explain how teaching is organised)

14 What levels do you teach?

15 How do you assess your pupils?

16 How do you recognise their achievements?

17 What resources do you provide for students?

18 What resources do you provide for teachers?

19 What qualifications do your students take?

20 What academic results did they achieve? (If applicable)

Use of the funds*

21 How much funding have you received from the EAZ?

22 What were your expectations as to how you might spend the money?

23 What have you spent it on?

24 How effective has the expenditure been?

25 What difference have the funds made to the teaching and learning of your pupils?

26 What difference have the funds made to teachers?

27 How many pupils are you expecting to enter for GCSEs this summer and in what subjects?

28 If money were available next year from the EAZ how would you spend it?

29 What support, if any, would you like from the LEA?

30 Are there any other comments you would like to make?

* The madrasahs which were visited with this interview schedule had each received a grant of £2000 through a mini education action zone (EAZ) based round Moat Community School, Leicester.

Box 25

Madrasahs and mainstream
– results and reflections from a survey

In 2003/04 Moat Community School, Leicester, provided through a mini education action zone small (£2000) grants to four madrasahs. Three of the madrasahs were visited by a researcher. Here is an account of his findings and reflections.

Attendance
All took pupils predominantly from the local area in which they were based but all also had pupils who travelled from across the city.

Buildings
Two were based in school premises, one in a large mainstream secondary school and the other in an independent Muslim school. The third had its own building, owned by the mosque to which it was attached.

Ethnicity of students
No one ethnic group was predominant. In two, Pakistani heritage pupils were in the majority, but other Muslims, including Somalis, other South Asian and African groups were also represented. The other contained a wider mix of pupils, the majority of whom were South Asian (Pakistani, Gujarati, and Bengali) and the remainder being of Somali or Arab heritage.)

Age and gender mix
All three took pupils from the age of four or five until fifteen and one continues until the pupils are sixteen. They all found that once students reached Year 10 in their mainstream school their attendance at madrasah declined markedly. Girls were in the majority of the madrasahs attached to the mosque; boys in the unattached school.

Fees
The unattached madrasah charged fees of £325 per annum, compared with £9.50-£10 per month in the others.

Class size
Class sizes averaged at about 20 pupils per class but in some cases could be as many as 25. Many of the classes were mixed aged, and were mixed gender for younger pupils. The numbers tended to decline as pupils got older possibly because the academic demands of mainstream schools became more demanding as students reached Years 10 and 11.

Time commitment
In school term time, most students spent one and half to two hours a day each week at the madrasah, depending on age. Most attended for ten hours each week, Monday through Friday. Two of the madrasahs started at 5pm and finished at 7pm. The third began at 5.55 and ended at 7.30. They did not open during Ramadan.

Curriculum and assessment
The nature of the curriculum was very similar for all three, except that one also taught English, maths and science to the older pupils. They all taught the Holy Qur'an, Muslim manners and customs, and Muslim history, Muslim jurisprudence, and Arabic. In addition, two taught some Urdu. The language of instruction depended on the nature of the subject taught, except for the youngest children where much of the teaching was in English. Instructional English was the main vehicle for much of the communication.

None of them had external syllabuses to follow. All had devised their own syllabuses, often using templates. All tested their own pupils, often with quite elaborate and detailed materials that the children had to learn by heart. All set examinations and had an elaborate system of tests that were designed to see if pupils had learnt key materials. Pupils had to learn a large range of materials in Arabic related to Islam including *wudu*, (ritual ablution prior to prayer), *kalimat* (the creed), *duas* (the supplications to Allah), and *surahs* (chapters of the Qur'an). They were taught how to undertake *salah/namaz* (prayers).

Pupils were normally provided with books in Arabic and history but they had to provide their own stationery, pens and pencils. More expensive books had to be provided by the parents because of the low level of central funding held by the schools.

Celebration of achievement
All three were very keen to acknowledge their pupils' achievements within their own institution. Typically pupils were rewarded with certificates, letters of encouragement, head teacher's awards and trophies. One involved the parents closely, and provided a parents evening with a detailed twelve page report on the progress of their charges. None informed the mainstream schools of the many and sometimes considerable achievement of their pupils. No formal methods of accreditation were utilised. It was considered that mainstream schools could incorporate

Box 25 continued

these successes in formal processes such as Records of Achievement

Teachers

Many of the teachers did not have any formal teaching qualifications. Generally however, the teachers did have teaching experience from which to draw on. Most of the untrained teachers were women, often acting in an unpaid capacity. Some had alims and alimas working for them. These were men and women of knowledge, scholars, especially in the Islamic sciences. They had been trained for up to seven years at a Dar-Ul-Alooms, normally abroad, and could genuinely be said to be experts in the field. Some had one or more hafiz on their books also. They had spent up to four years memorising the whole Qur'an by heart.

One of the schools had weekly staff meetings where teaching methodology was discussed, and practical examples of lesson delivery offered. Team meetings were also held. The others relied upon classroom visits from the principal for feedback on their teaching performance and attended other training, when it became available. There was little systematic training in pedagogy.

Support from the City Council

Unsurprisingly they were keen for support to continue after EAZ funding ended. In particular they wanted help with rent and teacher salaries. They also saw some real advantages in developing ICT capabilities, especially in developmental areas like Arabic, as well as in the purchase of hardware. All three were more than aware of the positive contribution their madrasah could make to community cohesion. The principal of the oldest madrasah articulated a very well worked programme, which, with sufficient funding, he believed could make a serious difference to the educational attainment of Pakistani heritage pupils. For him, the key was parental participation, without which he believed the Pakistani community would fall even further behind than at present. A combination of madrasahs, the City Council, external consultants and other experts could help overcome these barriers.

Far from being isolationist in any way, all three were very keen to develop closer links with the City Council. They saw this survey and a forthcoming city-wide conference sponsored by the DfES Innovations Unit and organised by the City Council as a positive affirmation of their work.

They stressed, as one headteacher put it: 'Before we were like aliens in the system, doing our job and no one knew what we were doing here. I think this [the closer relationship] is a very positive thing... I can tell you with confidence that madrasahs... are making good citizens of Britain.'

Conclusion

From this small survey it is clear that the modest amount of finding received from the IMPACT EAZ has made an immediate difference in terms of the purchase of extra books and equipment, and the payment to teachers (especially teachers of Arabic). In the longer term, all three hoped to introduce Arabic GCSE with their Year 10 students. Far from being exclusive and isolationist, they were all very keen to have far closer links with mainstream education than at present. They could see and valued the potential benefits to their pupils if these links could be systematically encouraged through open and unprejudiced dialogue.

Source: paper by Maurice Irfan Coles, 2004

less dramatic for the girls at KS3 and KS4. Those who do attend, however, are there for considerable amount of time. Although there is no comparative data for KS1and 2, evidence collected in visits to madrasahs (see box 25) indicates that all their charges, including the youngest, spend up to two hours every day throughout the working week in the madrasahs in term time.

The principal of Moat Community School was faced, therefore, with a clear challenge. She resolved to transform it into an opportunity. Many of her Muslim pupils were obviously devout and mosque and madrasah attendance was an important part of their identity. How could an individual school build upon the work the madrasahs were doing so that overall pupil attainment was raised? The solution was essentially simple. She wrote to a number of complementary schools in the area and offered to support them in their teaching and learning by providing a £2000 grant per year for three years. To secure receipt they were only required to do two things:

☐ provide a simple written record of how they had spent the money e.g. on teachers, books, resources

☐ enter their pupils for GCSE or other examinations in their local secondary school in the subjects they studied at the madrasah or in their complementary school.

Four madrasahs and one African Caribbean institution responded to the initial letter but the latter was unable to take up the offer.

The term complementary school has recently replaced the terms supplementary school and community school in order to stress that such provision, actually or potentially, has a key role to play in partnership with mainstream schools.[2] In the Muslim communities complementary schools are known as 'madrasahs', which literally means places of study. Often, though not always, madrasahs are part of a mosque and are therefore sometimes referred to as mosque schools. The mosques often subsidise the classes.

In order to gain a more accurate picture of madrasahs in modern Britain a researcher visited three of the madrasahs supported by Moat Community School, Leicester, as outlined above. The interview schedule he used was developed by Birmingham University and Leicester University and is shown in box 24. It shows the kind of question that all schools and LEAs arguably need to ask about the complementary education which their students are receiving through mosques and madrasahs. There is a summary of findings in box 25.

Local education authorities

Leicester is by no means the only LEA to have worked closely with complementary schools. Another excellent example can be found in Kirklees which in 2003 published their *Safe Children Sound Learning Guidance for Madressahs*. This was written as a result of joint work between the Lifelong Learning and Social Affairs and Health departments. The publication, aimed at the 50 madrasahs and supplementary schools throughout the LEA, includes straightforward and accessible guidance on behaviour management, child protection, roles and responsibilities, health and safety and recruitment and training. It provides a comprehensive overview on most issues related to effective complementary schooling.

The Birmingham Advisory and Support Service (BASS) has worked closely with the city's diverse range of complementary schools.[3] Employing Standards Fund money, it offers a comprehensive training package, which is classroom focused and includes, amongst other things, components on classroom management, teacher assessment, pupil participation and developing links with mainstream schools. Courses are delivered in the evenings and on Saturdays in recognition that many complementary schoolteachers have other jobs in working hours. The package builds on the work already undertaken by the Education Department's Equalities Unit, which had organised six local ward forums into an overarching Birmingham Supplementary Schools Forum with its own administration and website.[4]

Few would argue that the complementary sector forms an important part of the overall provision that pupils receive. There has, however, been little UK based research into the effectiveness of these schools. However, the universities of Leicester and Birmingham, working closely with the LEA, produced a preliminary report on complementary schools and their communities in Leicester in June 2003. This was

followed by a significant piece of research by Bhatt, Martin and Creese based on a close study of two Gujarati schools, which found that complementary schools enhance learning and literacy; reinforce or complement other educational practices, for example with regard to discipline and citizenship; and support pupils' choices and development of identities.[3]

The local and national picture formed the general background for a project in Leicester coordinated by the School Development Support Agency (SDSA). An interim board was set up with the task of securing funding for a full time Complementary Schools Coordinator and a long term Leicester Complementary Schools Trust. The board members were chosen from a range of complementary schools, the University of Leicester and mainstream schools. The purpose was to bring the sector together, enhance its relationship with mainstream schools, and offer support, help and guidance in all matters related to complementary education. The interim trust deed, shown in Box 26, may be a valuable model or basis for discussion in other LEAS.

Working with imams

Another form of partnership between school and mosque has been developed at a school in the London Borough of Redbridge. The majority of students is Muslim. In 1999 five per cent of all students gained 5 A*-C grades but this improved to 67 per cent in 2003, making the school the ninth most successful secondary school in terms of value-added in England. One of the reasons behind this dramatic turnaround was the involvement of two local imams in a mentoring scheme for Year 11 students. There is a description of the scheme in box 27.

In the light of experiences in a range of local authorities it is possible to draw up lists of advice, guidance and tips for fostering good working relationships between the statutory sector (LEAs and schools) and the complementary sector, including madrasahs. Based on experience in Leicester, there are three such lists in box 28.

Box 26

Strengthening the complementary sector
– a draft trust deed

Name
Leicester City Complementary Schools Trust

Aim
To raise attainment and achievement by improving the quality of teaching and learning in all the City complementary schools.

Objectives
1   To act as an advocate for the range of complementary provision, with a view to maximising mutual support and development.

2   To discover the training and development needs of complementary staff.

3   To devise and deliver training and development programmes to meet these needs.

4   To develop a shared quality complementary school standards framework, against which the City's complementary schools can be monitored.

5   To support complementary schools in their self-evaluation processes.

6   To facilitate links between complementary schools, mainstream colleagues and other stakeholders.

7   To communicate information about local and national initiatives.

8   To receive progress reports from the Development Worker.

9   To offer support, guidance and strategic direction to the Development Worker.

10 To identify sources of sustainable income.

11 To celebrate and highlight the work of Leicester's complementary schools.

12 To support the organisation and administration of existing and new complementary schools.

Source: Leicester City Council February 2004

Box 27

Raising achievement through mentoring
– the involvement of imams

Programme
The mentoring scheme was led by two local imams. It involved them visiting the school, meeting the identified students in small groups to discuss their attitudes to education, work/ and study patterns and aspirations for the future; talking to students in lessons; and through an assembly programme exploring major festivals in world religions. Following the mock GCSE exams, suggestions for further development were made.

Impact on results
In the GCSE examinations at the end of the year, the results of Muslim students (whether or not they were in the mentored group) were remarkable compared with national averages. Sixty-four per cent of Pakistani-heritage students achieved 5 A*-C grades, compared with 30 per cent nationally. Relationships between the students and staff also improved. The headteacher considered that the self-esteem of the students had risen when they had seen their own community representatives being recognised by the school and that this self-esteem had in its turn led to confidence in their own ability to study, learn and achieve good results.

Student perspectives
The mentored students were surveyed by questionnaire to help evaluate the scheme's impact. Their responses showed:

☐ The majority found the imams to be encouraging

☐ The majority of students thought that the mentoring sessions helped to improve their attitude to work and study

☐ Significant comments were that they found it 'comfortable to talk to someone from our own background', that 'authority figures make us work' and that it was beneficial 'talking to someone from outside school'.

☐ Utilising the Imams' experience and influence in the community was seen as positive, for they provided a link between the school and home. Imams are important, respected members of the Islamic community, so if the Imam visits the school and tells the students that school is important then the students will think school is important too.

☐ All thought that the mentoring sessions should be repeated for the next year's group.

The second year
It was agreed to continue with the mentoring scheme during 2002-2003 with a new cohort of students. Suggested improvements to the scheme from the mentored students included:

☐ Increased mentoring time and frequency of sessions, especially when exams are imminent so the imams could assist with exam preparation

☐ More liaison between the school and the imam so the Imam can support the school by stressing its importance at events at the mosque

☐ Additional clubs such as Maths or Science club to help improve grades

☐ Use of Muslim businesspeople as they are also an integral part of the community.

The school decided to produce clear guidance for the mentors on their role and the mentoring process and trained the imams in target-setting and the use of data to help raise underachievement. The school also arranged a special evening for Punjabi and Urdu speaking parents to build links with some of the harder to reach parents. The school newsletter is now produced in these community languages. A female Muslim Education Welfare Officer was employed to work with groups of parents, often mothers with minimal fluency in English. Ofsted commented in their inspection of the school in 2003: 'There is a very positive ethos which embraces inclusion of all, regardless of race, religion or social background.'

Source: London Borough of Redbridge, autumn 2003

Box 28

Partnerships and principles
– mainstream and the complementary sector working together

Points for mainstream schools

1   Be aware and empathise with complementary schools. Some may be suspicious of your motives, and may be concerned that you are trying to take them over. Be sensitive to this in any approach you may make.

2   Stress the complementarity of your aims. Mainstream and complementary schools exist to support the individual in their attempt to attain and achieve more and in responding to the cultural, religious and linguistic needs of their students.

3   Conduct a school based audit and ask your pupils:
    Who attends complementary schools?
    Which schools do they attend?
    When do they go?
    How often do they attend?
    What subjects do they study there?
    How are their achievements celebrated?
    Do they undertake any formal examinations?

4   Make contact with all or, if there is a large number, the main complementary schools in your area. Explain that the school would appreciate closer links in the long term interest of the pupils.

5   Create a mutually supportive ethos. Ascertain if the school can help with meeting any of the training or organisational needs of the complementary school.
    If possible, offer some financial support.
    If possible, offer premises at a nominal cost after school.

6   Use the extended school funds if you already have them, or consider making a bid on any money centrally held in this category.

7   Ask if the school can help celebrate pupil achievement in the sector, for example through assemblies, records of achievement, or any other of the school's normal processes for recognising achievement.

8   If you are a secondary or 6th form college suggest that pupils take their formal qualifications at your centre. This serves the dual purpose, hopefully, of increasing your students' GCSE tally and increasing the school's own number of 5 A*-Cs.

9   Ask your LEA what their policy and practice is towards the complementary sector.

Points for local authorities

1   Conduct an audit of complementary schools in your area.

2   Try to match up complementary with mainstream provision. From which feeder schools do children come for their complementary education?

3   Discuss with these schools the possibilities and advantages of forming closer links with the complementary sector

4   Ascertain whether there are already in your LEA examples of good practice on which to build

5   Allocate responsibility for overseeing the authority's work with the complementary sector

6   Develop a council policy for complementary education

7   Explore avenues of funding and support locally, regionally and nationally

8   Support the sector by attending their achievement functions and develop an authority wide celebration event

9   Formally encourage complementary schools to enter their pupils for GCSE and other examinations at your local centres

10 Offer maximum support, advice and help in the setting up, maintaining and smooth running of the sector

11 Develop training packages of support in partnership with the sector to enhance the quality of the teaching ands learning

12 Consider working in formal partnership with the complementary schools by establishing a trust to oversee development

Box 28 continued

Partnerships and principles
– mainstream and the complementary sector working together

Points for complementary schools

1　Ask your LEA about their policy for complementary schools

2　Enquire about what funding is available to support you

3　Discover if there is any training and other kinds of support on offer

4　Find out if there is a forum or trust or similar body in the authority that is designed to support you. If so, make contact. You may wish to consider joining it.

5　Consult your local councillors about funding and support

6　Conduct a pupil audit to discover which schools your pupils attend

7　Write to the Headteacher of the schools with large numbers of pupils in order to see what help, support and advice they might be able to offer you

8　Encourage your staff to attend training offered by the LEA

9　Discover and if necessary purchase the various documents already on offer to support you in the smooth running of your school.

Source: from a paper by Maurice Irfan Coles

8 THEY CAN'T JUST STAND THERE
– training and preparing staff

SUMMARY

Chapter 8 describes how a secondary school in Rotherham set about preparing for a major change in its student population. There is a reference to a staff conference; various handouts and guidelines to help staff with everyday incidents; and interviews with students and parents. The chapter is based on a paper by Mary Sculthorpe, who is the EMA coordinator at Kimberworth School, Rotherham. At the time that the paper was written, Kimberworth was in the process of merging with Old Hall School.

Are there specific skills, strategies, insights and understandings that teachers need to have and to use in schools which have substantial numbers of Pakistani heritage learners? If so, what are they? And how are they developed? These questions are particularly apposite and urgent when a school's pupil population changes quite suddenly, for example as a result of merging with another school.

In 2003, for example, Howard School in the suburbs of a northern city merged with Morris School in the centre.[1] At Howard, before the merger, there were no Pakistani heritage learners and indeed virtually none at all who are not, in the term of the census, 'white-UK'. At Morris, however, 20 per cent of the learners were not 'white-UK'. Most of these had English as an additional language and many were of Pakistani heritage. The head and senior staff of the new school wished to ensure that the staff would be equipped to work in a linguistically and culturally diverse school in which the needs of Pakistani heritage pupils are recognised and met. They were clear that there was a need for:

☐ improved staff understanding of the varied needs of Pakistani heritage pupils

☐ improved staff confidence in their ability to develop strategies which would positively impact on the learning and attainment of Pakistani heritage pupils

☐ increased involvement of Pakistani heritage parents and community members

☐ increased pupil confidence that their needs would be recognised and met

Some Pakistani heritage parents were interviewed during the preparatory period and their comments and anxieties were taken seriously and fed back to staff in both schools. They included:

> Somebody told me that children there [i.e. the new school] are a bit naughty, they not like coloured children.

> Teachers can only teach if they've got a relationship, they've got to be able to communicate, they can't just stand there and not know the children's personal backgrounds... I don't know how much they know about our children's backgrounds. Is it gonna be, 'all black faces, they're all Pakis'?

Inset day

As far as most staff were concerned, plans for the multicultural nature of the new school began to take shape at an inset day held in January 2003, nine months before the new school would open. The day was entitled Preparing for Cultural Diversity. There was a keynote address and then most of the day was spent in workshops. The topics and titles of these were:

☐ Diversity across the curriculum

☐ Racial harassment in schools

☐ Language, literacy and culture

Box 29

We must raise the level of debate – reflections and plans

The keynote address
Hit a few nerves – we must raise the debate at all levels
Made me think an awful lot in a slightly different way
Raised general issues but started you thinking of your own situation
Too long, too many metaphors, uncertain of relevance to the topic

Workshops
Promoted real awareness
Made me question my ideas and think about my heritage
Interesting ideas for working with bi-lingual pupils in the classroom
Good overview of legal standpoint and policy
I learned so much about the community I will be working with.
Extremely relevant to the classroom situation
Excellent – lots of real experiences highlighted.
Made you think of aspects of planning lessons
Walking on eggshells with some staff
Developed confidence about my ability to manage situations
Too much information and input – more time needed for interaction
Questions raised – not enough answers given
Need more practical advice on specific ways of combating racism
More practical applications would be appreciated

Final Plenary Session
Good to get permission to get things wrong
A good start has been made
What we are facing is not a problem but an opportunity
It's an exciting prospect. I am looking forward to learning from it
We need to spend much longer on these issues – addressing them in whole school and departmental groups
This needs to be the beginning of an ongoing programme
Source: comments on evaluation sheets at a staff conference

☐ The Race Relations (Amendment) Act 2000 and implications for schools

☐ Teaching students who have English as an additional language

☐ Addressing expectations, hopes and fears, and

☐ Antiracist education and the global dimension.

Box 29 shows the kind of feedback that staff wrote on their evaluation forms at the end of the day.

Following the conference there were several follow-up activities. These included a working party to draft a policy statement in accordance with the Race Relations (Amendment) Act; the provision of guidelines for all staff on various issues; several twilight training sessions; and interviews and meetings with parents and students, and with Year 6 pupils in feeder primary schools.[2] Further, the school was closely involved in a local forum on community cohesion and education. The forum had teacher, governor and parent governor representatives from local secondary schools, and from the LEA, the council, the youth service, South Yorkshire Police and the race equality council.

Guidance papers
In the production of guidance papers, an initial priority was to signal to staff that there would be much diversity amongst the new students, for the term 'minority ethnic' refers to a wide range of identities, histories and experiences. So some brief profiles were compiled of individual students. Box 30 shows the form they took.

Box 30

Where they're coming from – notes on some students

Eva is in year 7. She was born in the UK, and has had all her education here. Her parents are from Hong Kong, the home language is Cantonese. She is very reserved with adults, but quietly confident, and much more lively with her friends.

Miriam is in year 8. She was born in the UK and has had all her education here. She has dual Yemeni/English heritage, and balances her two cultures confidently, celebrating Eid and Christmas. English is her first and stronger language.

Farid is in year 9. He came to seek asylum here from Afghanistan in May 2001 with his older brother. The rest of the family are in Pakistan. Although his brother has been given leave to remain for three more years, Farid is still awaiting a decision on his own case. He wants passionately to be a doctor and has chosen his GCSE options with that in mind. His first language is Dari and he also speaks Farsi, Pushto and Urdu. He is Muslim, but is vehemently opposed to the extremism of the Taliban.

Sueado is in year 10. She and her mother came from Somalia in October 2000 to join her father who had already fled the country four years earlier. Her first language is Somali, but she does not read or write it. Her first 'school language' is Italian, and she has just taken Italian GCSE a year early. She is a Muslim with a western approach to life, continuing to grow in confidence socially and academically.

Habib is in year 11. He was born in the UK, the youngest son of a now quite elderly widowed mother. His father died when he was in year 8 and he made a lengthy return visit to Pakistan. He is a Muslim but no longer attends the mosque school. His first language is Mirpuri-Punjabi and he understands Urdu but has opted for Spanish as his GCSE language.

Habib is able to describe what has helped him at school:

- ☐ The use of memorable visual examples – in a Maths lesson, pupils themselves 'modelled' mode, median, mean and range.

- ☐ Careful explanation, slowly and with repetition, on the board using words and diagrams.

- ☐ Working with a friend you can help and be helped by, using English and Mirpuri – Punjabi.

- ☐ Learning that words can have more than one meaning, 'Before we did osmosis, I thought solid just meant baby food!'

- ☐ Having older sisters who've been through the system.

- ☐ Linking new ideas with something you already know 'Like witches at Hallowe'en and in Macbeth'

- ☐ Parental encouragement and support.

Source: training material at a secondary school in Rotherham

Cultural Awareness

Many staff were nervous about unintentionally offending the new students and requested some simple do's and dont's. The EMA coordinator went along with the request because she thought the advantages of winning colleagues' trust and respect outweighed the dangers of generalising and over-simplifying, and maybe even stereotyping. Box 31 shows one of the drafts that she prepared.

Box 31

Cultural awareness – some frequently asked questions

Why do some pupils seem to avoid eye-contact?
Don't misunderstand some (not all) pupils' failure to look you in the eye. Downcast eyes are in fact a sign of respect for adults in many cultures.

I usually shake hands with parents when I meet them.
Many Muslims (not all) feel uncomfortable shaking hands with members of the opposite sex.

Are there rules about Muslim dress?
Most Muslim girls are not allowed to wear clothes which expose their skin or body shape. Many would also prefer to wear the hijab, or headscarf, if not in school then at least on the way to and from school.

What do I need to know about food?
Muslims cannot eat food that is not halal, and never eat pork, or any product derived from pork (eg gelatine) In general, this means that they will choose vegetarian options if they have school dinners, or if they are cooking in a food technology lesson. Alcohol is also forbidden.

What happens during Ramadan?
During the month of Ramadan most Muslim children of secondary age will fast during daylight hours. This means they have nothing to eat or drink, nothing should enter their mouths. They are proud of this abstinence, which teaches them self-control and what it means to be hungry. Understandably, returning home to 'open the fast' at the end of the day is very important.

How often do pupils go to the mosque?
Most younger (up to 13 or 14) Muslim pupils attend classes at the mosque school, (madrassa) for one or two hours every evening, usually as soon as they get home from school. They will therefore start their homework later in the evening, after the evening meal. Many will take advantage of pre-school and lunchtime homework clubs. Older boys may also be expected to attend Friday prayers, especially if they have been on Haj (pilgrimage to Mecca)

Why do some pupils have such long periods of condoned absence?
Many families arrange extended visits to Pakistan for their children, often during the school holidays. They are understandably concerned to maintain family links, and the visits play a crucial part in developing pupils' sense of their roots and self-identity. If they miss weeks of term time, pupils will need support to catch up, but it is also important to recognise what they have gained, and to give them the opportunity to share their experiences when they return.

What do I need to be aware of when grouping pupils?
Some pupils may prefer to work in single sex groups for PHSE when discussing sensitive issues.

Some pupils seem to 'switch off' in class.
Listening to an unfamiliar language is tiring. Support pupils' concentration by speaking clearly, using short sentences and repeating important points and instructions.

Should we insist that pupils only speak English in lessons?
Many pupils (not just 'beginners') benefit from using their first language in the classroom. They may need reminding to use it appropriately, but if they are not given the opportunity to use it positively they may well react by using it negatively.

I think she understands, but she hardly says a word!
Many pupils in the early stages of learning another language go through a 'silent period.' They will build up confidence by working in pairs or small groups, either with pupils who share the same first language (who will themselves benefit) or with competent native English speakers whom they can imitate. They can also be given opportunities to demonstrate their understanding in non-verbal ways.

Source: handout for staff at a school in Rotherham, 2003

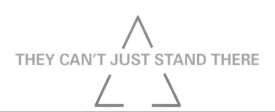
Dealing with racist incidents

There was anxiety amongst Pakistani heritage parents, as outlined at the start of this chapter, that staff at the new school might be inexperienced in dealing with racist incidents. To assist and support the school on this extremely important matter, and also all other schools in Rotherham, the LEA issued a guidance document. It drew on similar documents issued in other LEAs and contained at one stage a set of principles. These are shown in box 32.

The abstract principles set out in box 32 need to be illustrated and internalised at staff training sessions through discussion of real or imaginary situations and events. Box 33 provides some examples based on real events in the period 2001-2003.[1]

Box 32

Principles for dealing with racist incidents
– guidance for schools

1. Always do something
It is tempting when faced with comparatively minor expressions of racist behaviour to think that ignoring them might be the best course, arguing that to react might be to highlight the racism and make matters worse. Racism feeds on the inactivity of non-racist people. It must be confronted on every occasion. The judgement to be made is about the appropriate way to confront it.

2. Consider the victim(s) first
In considering what is the appropriate action to take think first of the feelings and needs of the victims. They need to be supported but again in an appropriate way. For instance, harsh public attacks on the perpetrator and public expressions of sympathy for the victims may bring about more embarrassment and hurt. They need to be quietly assured by the words and actions of staff that they are valuable members of the community of the school; and that racial harassment will not be tolerated. Clear guidance should be given about what steps to take should anything like it occur again.

3. Look to help the perpetrator
It must be made clear to the perpetrator also that racist behaviour and racial harassment will not be tolerated and that appropriate sanctions will be applied, including exclusion if necessary. However, in the longer term the school should look to address the racist attitudes that underlie the harassment. Formal or informal counselling in a caring atmosphere or addressing issues in a circle time exercise is likely to bear more fruit than attempting to instil fear or guilt.

4. Consider whether there other people who need to be involved
Racist behaviour of children and young people may well be repeating behaviour they have learned from home or outside of school. It may then be appropriate to involve their parents or guardians in discussion following an incident so that they are clear what will not be tolerated by the school and so that they may be involved in the educational process of the young people. It may also be a good thing to liaise with the parents of the victims to ensure that they are aware of the support that their children might need and to assure them that the school is taking appropriate action.

5. Think about how the actions taken will be viewed on the public scene
While bearing in mind what is said above about the possible results of harsh public criticism for the perpetrator and public expressions of sympathy for the victim, if a racist incident has taken place on the public scene, that is before groups of other pupils, it needs to be clear to those pupils that the incident has not been ignored and that action has been taken. It may be more appropriate to speak to these pupils at a later time, without the presence of the victim or perpetrator, but they must see that the values proclaimed by the school are being upheld.

Source: Rotherham Education Authority, autumn 2003

Box 33

What happens next? – some stories and situations

A bit of teasing

I'm the only Asian teacher at my school. During the war in Iraq a pupil who's also Asian told me that she was being teased by other pupils. 'We killed hundreds of your lot yesterday ... Saddam's your dad, innit ... we're getting our revenge for what you Pakis did to us on 11 September...' I asked her if she had told her class teacher. Yes, she had told her teacher, and her teacher had said: 'Never mind, it's not serious. It'll soon pass. You'll have to expect a bit of teasing at a time like this.'

Wound me up

A Year 9 pupil was complaining to me bitterly earlier today. 'All right, I'm overweight and I'm not proud of it. But it really gets to me when other kids go on about it. Last week I lost it. I was out of order, right, but when these two kids said I was fatter than a Teletubby and twice as stupid I swore at them and used the word Paki. I got done for racism and was excluded for a day and my parents were informed and all, and I'm really pissed off, and nothing at all has happened to the kids who wound me up. It's not fair.'

Back door

As a secondary school governor I proposed, following discussions with pupils and parents, that there should be some Islamic Awareness classes at the school on a voluntary basis. 'We'd just be letting Al Qaida in by the back door,' said the chair. The other governors all seemed to agree, or anyway not to bother.

Not surprising

I mentioned to a pupil's mother that her son had made some unacceptably negative and extreme remarks about people seeking asylum. 'Well unfortunately it's not at all surprising,' she said. 'The fact is, my husband is an active member of the BNP.'

Unpatriotic

In my capacity as deputy head I photocopied an article in the current issue of the journal *Race Equality Teaching* on talking and teaching about the war in Iraq. I gave a copy to all staff and governors. The chair of governors has written to me saying that in his view the article is biased and unpatriotic and should be withdrawn immediately.

Get on with your work

In October 2001 I had occasion to observe a colleague's Year 8 RE lesson. The students were copying pictures of Hindu deities into their books. 'These are the people who crashed the planes into the twin towers, aren't they, miss' said a boy. 'No,' she replied. 'That was Muslims, we're doing Hindus. Just get on with your work.'

Images of the future

In a PSHE lesson I asked Year 9 students to draw sketches of themselves as they expected to be in 10 years time. All the Pakistani-heritage boys in the class drew themselves as Osama bin Laden, complete with Kalashnikov rifle.

Source: training materials based on real events, 2001-03

Interviews and discussions

Interviews and discussions with students played an essential part in the preparations for the new school. Their feelings about the merger and their views on racism, religion and personal identity were fed back to staff and helped to illustrate abstract principles. Staff developed a vivid sense of the insights and concerns of the young people for whom they were professionally responsible.

A similar role was played in staff training and discussions at schools in Manchester. A researcher interviewed Pakistani heritage girls about their perceptions of school and about their favourite subjects and lessons. The findings were fed back to their teachers and helped to underpin training on learning styles and accelerated learning.[4]

Elsewhere in this book there are extracts from interviews with Year 11 students (see chapters 5 and 11). The next chapter ('Cat have two mouses') starts with the conversations of Year 2 pupils.

9 CAT HAVE TWO MOUSES
– MOVING TO ACADEMIC ENGLISH

SUMMARY

For most British children of Pakistani-Kashmiri heritage, English is an additional language, not their mother tongue. When they start nursery or infant school they fairly quickly develop basic interpersonal communication skills in English, and soon appear to speak English as fluently as do children for whom English is the mother tongue. However, they do not as readily develop the kinds of formal, academic language that are required, both orally and in writing, for progress in the National Curriculum. Various kinds of focused intervention, therefore, are required. This chapter describes work in Derby and Kirklees. It is based on papers by Monica Deb, a member of the EMA service in Kirklees and Tania Sanders, a primary achievement coordinator for Derby City access service. There is also an extract from a paper written by staff at Howden Clough School, Leeds.

Two types of English

Young children at the earliest stages of learning English as an additional language use the same non-standard forms that mother tongue speakers do. 'Cat have two mouses,' remarks a child looking at a picture and in doing so she manages to use three non-standard pieces of English within the space of four words. She will quite quickly pick up rules about articles, the present tense of verbs and irregular plurals – within two years, at most, she will have basic, interpersonal, communicative skills (BICS) which are similar to those of all other children the same age.[1] It will be several more years, however, before she has cognitive, academic language proficiency (CALP). As a cat may have two mice, every school pupil develops, more or less swiftly and fluently, two registers of language, conversational and academic.

If you are learning English as an additional language it is a great help if your teachers pay special attention to the development of CALP. This chapter outlines a range of ways in which such special attention may occur.

It is appropriate to start by considering children at KS1. The *Talking Partners* programme developed in Bradford aims to accelerate language learning in young children in order to lessen the gap between conversational skills and academic proficiency. The focus is on improving speaking and listening skills. It is a ten week programme which consists of three 20-minute sessions a week, the equivalent of one hour a week intensive, structured language input in small groups. The recommended ratio is one adult to three pupils.

Two advisory teachers in Derby[2] attended a three-day course in Bradford for *Talking Partner* trainers and on their return to Derby it was agreed that the programme should be piloted in seven primary schools. The report that follows here is based on work with Year 2 pupils, all of them of Pakistani heritage. In order to test the hypothesis that the programme would make a difference, use was made of the nationally recognised Renfrew Action Picture Test.[3]

Six pupils were selected to take part. All had Mirpuri-Punjabi as their home language. Before the programme began, each pupil was tested individually using the Renfrew Action Picture Test. The results are shown in tables A and B. They then engaged in the programme over the following ten weeks. As soon as the programme finished the test was administered again and gains were measured. Six months later the test was

TABLE A – VOCABULARY SCORES before the programme

Pupil	Age on day of test		Score	Test age		Difference between test age and chronological age
Tariq	6 years	1 month	26.5	4 years	0-5 months	2 years 1 month
Maleiha	6 years	6 months	28.5	4 years	6-11 months	2 years
Shahid	6 years	0 months	30	5 years.	0-5 months	1 year
Khalida	6 years	8 months	32.5	5 years	6-11 months	1 year 2 months
Safina	6 years	2 months	29.5	5 years	0-5 months	1 year 2 months
Tanvir	6 years	6 months	33	6 years	0-5 months	6 months

TABLE B – GRAMMAR SCORES before the programme

Pupil	Age on day of test		Score	Test age		Difference between test age and chronological age
Tariq	6 years	1 month	20.	4 years	0-5 months	2 years 1 month
Maleiha	6 years	6 months	20.	4 years	0-5 months	2 years 6 months
Shahid	6 years	0 months	13.	3 years	6-11 months	2 years 6 months
Khalida	6 years	8 months	20	4 years	0-5 months	2 years 8 months
Safina	6 years	2 months	18	4 years	0-5 months	2 years 2 months
Tanvir	6 years	6 months	20	4years	0-5 months	2 years 6 months

administered again for a third time, in order to establish whether the gains made at the end of the programme had been sustained.

The first set of results was evaluated with regard to (a) vocabulary and (b) grammar. They showed that in both respects all the pupils were operating below their actual age. Vocabulary such as *postbox, mouse* and *stick* all caused difficulties. Grammatical errors included not using future and past tenses. It was in response to the question 'What has the cat just done?' that one pupil answered 'Cat have two mouses'. In addition to the three errors that are clear out of context there was also an error of tense. Another similarly used the wrong tense: 'Catching the mouse'. Three others did use the past tense, but incorrectly – they said *catched*, not caught. All six children, it is important to note, fully understood the question and produced correct content.

A comparison of table A with B shows that one of the children (Tariq) was 'behind' in vocabulary and grammar by precisely the same amount.[4] The other five children were even more 'behind' in their grammar than in their vocabulary. This was serious, for CALP is much more closely related to grammar than to vocabulary. If a focused intervention at the age of six could make a difference to children's grasp of standard grammar this would have clear implications for the improvement of their cognitive, academic language proficiency.

After the 10-week programme was over, the six children were given the same test and the results were analysed in the same way. In vocabulary, one child (Tariq) had made no gain. All the others had gained at least six months since the programme had started and one (Maleiha) had gained 18 months. The average gain was 14.5 months. In grammar, all six children had gained by at least six months and the average gain was 12.8 months. These results were consistent with Bradford's findings in relation to far larger samples of pupils, the average gain in Bradford being at least 12 months after a 10-week programme.

An analysis of the responses for semantic content showed an increase in average length of utterance. Safina, for example, when asked before the programme 'What is the girl doing?' said 'Cuddling the bear.' Both subject and auxiliary verb were absent.

Box 34

Talking to learn – key features of the Talking Partners project

Talking Partners forms part of an integrated approach to raise levels of attainment in Bradford schools. It aims to improve pupils' speaking and listening skills across the curriculum.

Talking Partners draws particular attention to the links between oracy and literacy. It was designed to give children the skills they need to address many of the explicit and implicit demands of the National Literacy Strategy.

It offers training to adults in schools and the community to work with children helping them to become more confident and competent users of English.

Trained partners work with small groups of children three times a week for twenty minutes. They provide structured activities which encourage and support pupils' developing use of English in a variety of situations.

The focus of the activities varies and is linked to work the pupils are doing in their classes. The small group setting provides a positive, supportive environment where children can hear and practise new language. The project helps them to gain the confidence to become independent learners.

Talking Partners was developed for children in reception classes up to Year 4, but the programme has now been extended to Year 6. The support is designed for all pupils, whatever their general ability. The aim of the support is to provide young bilingual pupils with additional focused opportunities to use English.

In school a teacher is appointed as coordinator for the Talking Partners programme.

This teacher administers start and end of programme assessments and helps the partners collect and organise resources . Sometimes the coordinator is also able to work with a Talking Partners group and this strengthens the school programme.

Headteachers are given full information and invited to discuss implications before their school embarks on training partners. The headteacher's role as manager of all activity in their school is crucial to the success and sustainability of the programme.

Source: Education Bradford, 2003

Ten weeks later she replied: 'The girl is cuddling her nice bear.' The responses were generally more detailed and contained more connectives (*and*, *because*, and *to* as an abbreviation of *in order to*) and adjectives (*nice*).

But would the progress be sustained over the next six months without any further intervention from the *Talking Partners* programme? To answer this question, the same test was administered six months later. In grammar, it was found that all six pupils had either maintained their progress or had continued to make further progress: three pupils sustained their progress, one had gained a further six months and one had gained a further twelve months. In vocabulary, five had maintained progress or had improved it, two of them strikingly by 18 months. The sixth (Safina) had regressed in vocabulary. Her answers on the three occasions were studied and compared, to see if there was a clue to the reason. But no firm conclusions could be drawn. It may be that certain keywords had

not lodged in her long-term memory. Alternatively, she was maybe simply having 'a bad day' when the test was administered for the third time. Or maybe she was simply bored?

Implications

This was a small-scale project but it was clearly successful enough to be worth repeating. If implemented widely at KS1 in schools where there are substantial numbers of Pakistani and Kashmiri heritage children, and if it were similarly successful, it could have a marked impact on children's progress and achievement, particularly if it were linked to the kinds of school-home liaison outlined in chapter 6. The first step is to establish whether, indeed, the same results are replicated elsewhere with larger samples.

The teachers in Derby who ran the scheme were already highly experienced and expert practitioners in the fields of language education and early years

education. Some of the success in Derby was probably due to this. Also there may have been a halo effect – some of the success may have been due to the children being conscious of getting extra attention rather than to the programme itself. But there is no doubt that the project was beneficial for the professional development of all those who were involved in it. Some, maybe most, of the investment was worthwhile in terms of the enhancement of staff expertise and awareness.

All specialist teachers of English as an additional language would benefit from *Talking Partners* training, as would all teaching assistants who have occasion to work with children developing as bilingual learners.

The key feature of the *Talking Partners* programme are summarised in box 34.

Writing in secondary schools

The Advanced Bilingual Learners' (ABL) Writing Project was commissioned as part of an Ofsted study of support for students in KS4 and post-16 who use English as an additional language.

Over three hundred pieces of writing were analysed to produce profiles of achievement and needs, and suggestions for diagnosis and intervention by teachers. The research was by Lynne Cameron, professor of applied linguistics at the University of Leeds and was published by Ofsted in 2003.[5] Its principal findings are summarised below.

Writing is a cross-curricular issue

For example, skills of generating and organising content in essay-type writing are required in history and geography as well as in English. The use of modal verbs (*should, could, might*,etc) to discuss hypotheses, predictions and possibilities is required in all subjects, as is accurate use of comparisons, plurals, articles, tenses, subject-object agreements, punctuation and spelling. The English department can appropriately provide leadership in the development of such skills but all other departments have a responsibility too.

Students need instruction on the use of source materials

They may need help in finding appropriate materials. Certainly they need to be taught how to adapt the genre, register and stance of the materials they draw on so that their own writing has consistency.

Students should be taught techniques of generating and organising content

For example, brainstorming, mind-mapping around key words, using personal experience, breaking down topics into sub-topics and organising ideas into logical linear sequences.

Students need instruction on paragraphing

The skill of knowing when the expression of a new idea requires a new paragraph needs to be taught directly, not left to chance.

There should be focused attention to enrichment of vocabulary and more complex grammar

For example, students should be taught how to expand phrases into subordinate clauses; to modify nouns with adjectives; to use signposting phrases and linking terms; to choose between words that have different nuances of meaning; and to link sentences together with non-finite clauses such as *after listing the reasons...* or *in agreeing to this...*

Students sometimes need individual corrective feedback

This is particularly the case where a student's first language is different from English in the use of articles, tenses, plurals and subject-object agreement.

Students benefit from guided self-evaluation

It is valuable if students study extracts from their own writing, using a simple proforma based on the points above.

Implementation of the recommendations from Professor Cameron's research is clearly time-consuming and requires specialist expertise and training. Most teachers of history, geography and science feel that they already have more than enough to do without taking on concerns for correct grammar, richer vocabulary and appropriate use of genre. One major source of assistance to them is partnership teaching. Box 35 is about partnership teaching in science lessons at a secondary school in Kirlees.

Box 35

Benefits and opportunities – partnership teaching in science

Howden Clough School in Leeds conducted a review of its use of partnership teaching in the science department. The benefits of the programme were listed as follows.

For the science staff
- [ ] exposure to new ideas, approaches and resources
- [ ] topics covered in more detail
- [ ] opportunity to realise that if lesson content was unclear to a colleague it would be difficult for students also
- [ ] taking on board the importance of key words and definitions
- [ ] support with resources, marking and classroom management
- [ ] greater differentiation
- [ ] more opportunities to check understanding

For the students
- [ ] much clearer about aims and objectives
- [ ] higher marks in tests, leading to greater confidence and self-esteem
- [ ] work marked more frequently
- [ ] revision methods improved
- [ ] being more focused
- [ ] receiving more help in practical lessons
- [ ] exposure to a wider range of teaching styles and methods
- [ ] greater requirement to discuss ideas and explain and justify answers

For the EAL specialists
- [ ] grasping new knowledge in science and discovering new ways of getting ideas across
- [ ] using more visual and kinaesthetic teaching styles
- [ ] developing greater flexibility
- [ ] becoming more aware of the need for clear objectives for each lesson
- [ ] being respected for one's professional expertise by both colleagues and students

Source: Howden Clough School, Kirklees

Teachers as researchers

The teachers involved in the *Talking Partners* project, as also those who took part in the partnership teaching activities referred to in box 35, were all engaged in action research. So were the teachers whose work is reported in box 36. In this instance the context was a programme of classroom action research for teachers of maths and science, organised by their LEA's EMA service. They were introduced to a range of practical ideas for helping bilingual learners in their classrooms and then each focused on one idea in particular and experimented with it in their own situation.

The introductory sessions and follow-up meetings for reflection and tuition all took place on the school premises – not, for example, at the professional development centre – and involved all members of the department. There are notes in box 36 on three of the projects that were undertaken, respectively on questioning, key words and peer support. In all projects use was made of the LEA's assessment scheme for English language development assessment (ELDA), in order to inform planning and differentiation.

Box 36

Classroom action research
– experiments with questioning, key words and peer support

Questioning

Distinctions were made between closed questions, option-posing questions and open questions:

> Is this a mammal? (*closed*)
>
> Is this a mammal or a reptile? (*option-posing*)
>
> What class does this animal refer to? (*open*)

It was found that one of the benefits of option-posing questions is that they model correct mathematical or scientific terminology and require students to use technical terms in their reply. Another is that they enable the teacher to identify misunderstandings. One of the great advantages of consciously using the full range of styles of question – closed, option-posing, open – was that there was an increase in student confidence, participation and enthusiasm.

Further, a focus on the teacher's styles of questioning led to recognition of the importance of students being able to put questions to each other, both in writing and orally. In order to ask questions they had to produce specialist language and to give thought to how to be as clear as possible. It was thought that processes of devising clear questions would help them to understand better the nature and purpose of questions in examination papers.

Key words

Teachers identified the key specialist terms that students need to understand and use. They displayed these in English and in heritage languages, and used transliterations into Roman script as well as the traditional script. Supporting visuals were added wherever appropriate. Focused and explicit attention to certain specialist words was paid in every lesson. Students were encouraged to use the key words and were praised for doing so. They began to expect that every lesson would entail learning new words and enjoyed using the words correctly.

In addition to specialist scientific and mathematical terms, attention was paid to words such as *name*, *describe*, *explain* and *discuss*.

It was found that students made increasing use of accurate language both in writing and in discussions. Activities involving accurate transfer of information, for example jigsaw groupings, were found to be particularly valuable.

Often words were displayed in corridors as well as classrooms and were a topic of conversation and interest amongst a wide spread of students, not only those for whom they were intended.

Teachers were aware that translations of key words can be problematic and noted that students would often include specialist English words when talking in their heritage language.

At departmental meetings it was agreed that the focused attention to key words had been extremely beneficial. There were clear implications for departmental budgets; for the deployment and use of EMA staff; and for storage and retrieval systems.

Groupings and peer support

It was considered vital, if students were to develop fluency in academic language, that they should frequently work in pairs and small groups rather than as individuals. Teachers experimented with various kinds of grouping, for example by scores on language proficiency tests, gender, ethnicity, personality and first language. Important findings were:

- ☐ Groupings should generally be determined by the teacher, not left to the preferences of the students

- ☐ Students should experience a variety of groupings

- ☐ Mixed ability groupings are particularly valuable

- ☐ Every group should contain at least one positive role model

- ☐ Jigsaw exercises, requiring students to impart information which only they know, maintain interest and give valuable opportunities for students to produce specialist terminology

- ☐ The rationale for discussion and peer support should be made clear; otherwise students are inclined to think that they are being invited to cheat, or else that it doesn't matter if the discussion goes off task into gossip and chat

- ☐ Most students needed training in discussion skills

- ☐ An ethos of peer support needed to be established from Year 7 onwards

- ☐ There needed to be an overall departmental policy on the vital importance of peer support and departmental training should continue to provide opportunities for sharing and reflecting on activities and exercises that had been effective.

Source: report by Monica Deb, Kirklees LEA, 2003

10 MANY VIEWS, ONE LANDSCAPE
– DEVELOPING THE CURRICULUM

SUMMARY

The Ouseley report on Bradford recommended that the LEA should revise, improve and advance the citizenship component of the national curriculum so that it covers issues of diversity, racism and rights. This chapter describes how the recommendation is being implemented and discusses its relevance to raising achievement. It is based on a report by Joyce Miller, who is a member of Education Bradford's inspection and advisory service.

Context and issues

The summer of 2001 saw what came to be known as 'disturbances in northern towns'. One of the places in the spotlight was Bradford. It was also in Bradford that the first of a series of reports on community cohesion was published.[1] One of the report's principal recommendations was about revising, improving and advancing the citizenship component of the National Curriculum so that it covers, to quote the report itself, 'diversity, differences, rights and responsibilities, particularly with regard to behaviour and respect for others irrespective of background, appearance, characteristics, social circumstances or status.'

The expected outcomes of this recommendation, as listed in the report, were daunting but appropriately ambitious:

☐ reduced racial tension in schools and communities

☐ reduced levels of racial harassment

☐ increased participation in cultural and events

☐ young people better informed about the District's cultures and religions.

The slogan for Bradford's bid in 2002 to be named European Capital of Culture was 'Many Views, One Landscape'. 'That neatly sums up,' writes an LEA officer, 'what we are aiming for in citizenship education – to recognise that we are part of one landscape and that each of us has a story, a role, a place and a vision for the future of this community within multi-cultural Britain.'[2]

'None of us involved in this work,' she continues, 'believes that we are providing quick solutions. Our aim is that as this curriculum becomes embedded in the work of our schools there will be decreasing racism and increasing respect and understanding, but none of this is easily measured and there will be no quantitative data to vindicate our work. Nonetheless, it is our conviction that this work can and will impact on pupils and their attitudes, values and behaviours and that it will, albeit indirectly, contribute to the raising of pupils' attainment through an affirmation of their identities and the communities from which they come, alongside a commitment to race equality which is based on a recognition that all human beings are equal and that all racist behaviour is intolerable in our schools and in society as a whole.'

Principles

The development of the enhanced citizenship curriculum for Bradford schools was divided into stages, based on phases within the school system. The first priority was to address the secondary curriculum, for the time was fast approaching when citizenship education would be a statutory requirement at KS3 and 4. The government's light touch approach gives schools great freedom in determining how citizenship should be taught and by whom. So the Bradford scheme would have to be relevant to a wide range of organisational arrangements. Some schools taught citizenship as a discrete subject with specialist staff. Others used extra-curricular and cross-curricular provision. First, therefore, a set of principles was agreed:

☐ The citizenship curriculum should be seen within the context of the whole school community and its ethos. The antiracist component, for example, must permeate the whole curriculum and be reflected in the vision, values and practices of the whole school.

☐ Citizenship is inseparable from values and attitudes. All teachers and pupils will have to reflect on this as part of the educational process.

☐ The new curriculum must be a 'do-able' curriculum. In this way it will increase teachers' confidence and competence.

☐ It must be based on a sound theoretical framework of teaching and learning and must be active, interesting, relevant, participative and democratic, so that learners share ownership of their learning and of assessment procedures.

The national programmes of study for citizenship include 'the diversity of national, regional, religious and ethnic identities in the United Kingdom and the need for mutual respect and understanding' at KS3 and 'the origins and implications of diverse identities'. The national terminology was bland in the extreme, particularly when viewed in the light of experiences and events in Bradford. The formal aims and objectives of citizenship education were accordingly expanded, as shown in box 37.

Statements of objectives, for example those that are set out in box 37, are necessarily abstract. They can be brought to life through suggestions and guidance about practical classroom activities, as for example in boxes 38 and 39.

The issues touched on in boxes 38 and 39 are complex, sensitive and controversial and make considerable demands on the professional skills of teachers. Nevertheless they cannot be avoided. Research from Northern Ireland[3] and into teaching about Judaism in England[4] has shown that simply learning about other people's religion and culture does not necessarily modify the misconceptions and negative stereotypes which pupils bring with them to lessons. There is a summary of findings in Northern Ireland in box 40.

Box 37

Key concepts and objectives
– a framework for citizenship education

By the end of Key Stage 3 students will:

☐ understand key concepts, including identity, community, diversity, equality, justice, prejudice, race, racism and stereotyping

☐ understand the background to diversity in demographic change in local, national and global contexts

☐ understand and demonstrate respect for diversity, knowing the origins, beliefs and values of different sections of the community

☐ understand that social cohesion can be subject to many influences, including socio-economic factors

☐ demonstrate their understanding of commonality as well as difference within local, national, international and global contexts

☐ possess skills in listening and conflict resolution

☐ articulate their vision of and their contribution to Bradford District in the future.

By the end of Key Stage 4 students will:

☐ understand key concepts, including discrimination, racism, social and economic justice, and cohesion

☐ have a comprehensive understanding of and respect for diversity

☐ identify what unites as well as divides groups of people

☐ have the ability to engage in informed debate about living in a multi-cultural society

☐ understand that the world is a global community

☐ possess skills in conflict resolution, negotiation and evaluation

☐ articulate their vision of and their contribution to Bradford District in the future.

Source: Education Bradford, 2002.

Box 38

How do they describe themselves?
– first steps in citizenship education

☐ In pairs, pupils discuss their names and what they say about them. What do their names mean?

☐ Use circle time to explore and discuss the different groups to which they belong. How do they describe themselves? Where are they from? What are they like? What do they like doing? What are they good at? What are their beliefs? How do they describe themselves to other people – at school, to friends, on their passports, abroad. What do they have in common? What are the differences amongst them?

☐ Ask them to draw 'My network', with themselves in the middle and all the people of influence in their lives around them. Explore these networks in the context of choices and control. We can't choose our parents or siblings – but we can choose our friends. What is the basis of these relationships? Talk about ways in which conflicts can arise within the network. How do we resolve them? Do we resolve them differently with our friends and our siblings? Explore different ways of resolving conflicts and why it is important to do that.

☐ Stimulate discussion by getting pupils to bring in special objects that are representative of something about their own identities. Can they produce – perhaps using ICT – an emblem to represent their identity? Create a class display showing their similarities and differences.

☐ Ask pupils to prioritise their identities – cultural, ethnic, national, regional and religious. Which are the most important to them? Can they offer any reasons to explain their priorities? Which identities do pupils share?

Source: curriculum guidance prepared in Bradford, 2003

Box 39

The meaning of community
– boundaries and migration

☐ Use interviews, photos, the local library, newspapers and community organisations to research local communities. What do we mean by 'community' and 'communities'? Where are their boundaries? Do we belong to more than one community? What is in the local community? What would you like to change about your local community? Can you do anything about it?

☐ Why do people live in the Bradford District? Why have people migrated here from other places or countries? When? Explore the history of migration to Bradford. Where have people come from? Emphasise the fact that people have been coming to this area for a long time, including Jews, Ukrainians, Irish and others. What was and is the experience of people arriving in Bradford?

☐ Use personal stories, speakers and video recordings to illustrate people's experiences. Can pupils create an anthology of people's stories – including perhaps examples from their own families – to share with the class?

☐ How did and how does the 'host' community respond to changes in the population? Key areas include housing, employment and schools. Explore racism, including unintentional racism. What is prejudice? What are its causes? How can it be dealt with? What would a racially just and fair society look like?

☐ What are the benefits of living in a multi-ethnic community? Responses may include the sharing of culture, art, music and food as well as the contributions new groups make to local employment and services. Are there differences between the older generation and young people's attitudes to multicultural living?

☐ In 2002 Bradford made a bid to become European Capital of Culture. Prepare a presentation, including visual images, to convince people in your area or community that Bradford could win such a bid.

Source: adapted slightly from curriculum guidance in Bradford, 2003

Box 40

Contacts between schools
– points from experience in Northern Ireland

Research with school pupils and students in Northern Ireland has shown that the contacts between schools that serve different communities can be valuable if the following conditions apply:

☐ There is 'single identity work' as well. This involves members of a single community exploring their own identities, hopes and anxieties and relating these to the views they hold of non-members. Such work may be a valuable prelude to contact with the outgroup, or may alternatively accompany and complement such contact. Either way it needs to examine issues of gender identity as well as ethnic, religious and cultural identity, and needs to adopt a holistic approach to adolescent concerns and to peer-group pressures.

☐ Contact is part of a multi-layered approach – there is attention not only to the perceptions, stories, biographies and day-to-day experiences of individuals but also to the wider social processes and narratives in which these are interpreted and perpetuated.

☐ There is equal status between groups when they meet.

☐ Participants are involved in a cooperative venture with common goals, not for example in a win-lose situation such as a sports fixture.

☐ The contact has institutional support.

☐ It is accepted that conflict and misperception are 'inter-generational', namely that they are of long standing and are passed from one generation to another. Short-term interventions are not enough.

Source: Islamophobia: issues, challenges, and action, *Trentham Books 2004*

The citizenship curriculum in Bradford is complemented by several other projects. One of these is a schools linking project which brings together primary pupils from different backgrounds in a neutral environment over a sustained period to engage together in joint curriculum projects. Another is an RE and Citizenship project, in collaboration with the Professional Council for Religious Education and involving three other LEAs. Its aim is to enable secondary students to engage in dialogue on issues to do with Christianity and Islam. As well as conducting dialogue with each other, both face-to-face and by email, they talk with their parents and grandparents to develop their own personal story. They then explore their sense of identity and community further by sharing their story with students whose backgrounds and situations differ from their own.[5]

Consultation

Critical comment on the enhanced citizenship curriculum is sought at every stage of its development. Advice and suggestions have come not only from teachers but also from the Qualifications and Curriculum Authority, a member of Her Majesty's Inspectorate, the Bradford Interfaith Centre and the local SACRE.

It was the last group to be consulted that raised the most serious reservations, the Student SACRE. It members are sixth form students drawn from a range of different schools and communities and its role, like that of the official SACRE, is to advise the LEA on religious education and related matters. The students' main concerns were around issues of identity. What does the concept mean? Why has it been given such prominence?

As indicated in boxes 38 and 39, notions of identity and community inevitably lie at the heart of citizenship education. The students were uncomfortable with them because they suspected there was a hidden agenda. Was citizenship to do with the infamous Tebbitt test, they wondered – was there going to be stress on a single notion of British identity and would they be expected to renounce their Muslim, Pakistani, Kashmiri and South Asian identities? Would they be criticised, overtly or tacitly, if they said in lessons or in written work that their Muslim identity was as important as, or more important than, their British

---

Box 41

Closed and open views of Islam and 'the West'
– some key distinctions in citizenship education

When and how is it legitimate for non-Muslims to disagree with Muslims? How can you tell the difference between legitimate disagreement and phobic dread and hatred? To answer such questions, an essential distinction needs first to be made between what may be called closed views of Islam and open views. 'Phobic' hostility towards Islam is the recurring characteristic of closed views. Legitimate disagreement and criticism, as also appreciation and respect, are aspects of open views.

In summary, the distinctions between closed and open views are to do with:

☐ whether Islam is seen as monolithic, static and authoritarian, or as diverse and dynamic with substantial internal debates

☐ whether Islam is seen as totally 'other', separate from the so-called West, or as both similar and interdependent, sharing a common humanity and a common space

☐ whether Islam is seen as inferior, backward and primitive compared with the so-called West, or as different but equal

☐ whether Islam is seen as an aggressive enemy to be feared, opposed and defeated, or as a

cooperative partner with whom to work on shared problems, locally, nationally and internationally

☐ whether Muslims are seen as manipulative, devious and self-righteous in their religious beliefs, or as sincere and genuine

☐ whether Muslim criticisms of the so-called West are rejected out of hand or whether they are considered and debated

☐ whether double standards are applied in descriptions and criticisms of Islam and the so-called West, or whether criticisms are even-handed

☐ whether no account is made of the fact that Muslims have far less access to the media than non-Muslims, and are therefore at a competitive disadvantage on an uneven playing-field, or whether unequal freedom of expression is recognised

☐ whether anti-Muslim comments, stereotypes and discourse are seen as natural and 'common sense', or as problematic and to be challenged.

Source: Islamophobia: issues, challenges, and action, *Trentham Books 2004*

---

identity? Declarations of their identity, they feared, might be used against them.

British society has in fact never been homogeneous. On the contrary, it has been riven with disputes and conflicts, often violent, around differences of class, region, nation and religion.[6] But this reality is not well known to young people, whatever their ethnicity. So many – including in Bradford the communities of Pakistani and Kashmiri heritage – have an uneasy relationship with so-called mainstream society as they seek to accommodate competing claims on them and to shape and choose a coherent identity. It is not an easy process to conduct with integrity, given its huge complexity and given that the students are still young.

A second set of concerns came in particular from consultation with the official SACRE. The initial documents on citizenship education, it was pointed out,

did not refer by name to specific communities in Bradford. Nor did they refer to what many Muslims in Bradford (as elsewhere in Britain) consider to be the single most serious and urgent problem that they face, namely Islamophobia. Rather, the documents referred in general terms to local, national and global trends and of race, human rights and demographic change. One of the consequences of the community consultation with SACRE was the decision to teach explicitly about Islamophobia. Such teaching involves, amongst other things, distinguishing between 'open' views of Islam and 'closed'. There is an explanation of this distinction in box 41.

A third set of criticisms came from groups working in the field of antiracist education. The initial documents were considered to be unacceptably bland and non-explicit. Only if it is named and analysed, the argument ran, can racism in its various forms be addressed, reduced and removed. For example, there needs to be critical attention to the concept of 'race' and pupils need to learn that race is a social construct not a scientific one. Further, they need to study the roots of modern racism in the rise of European empires in the 18th and 19th centuries. Perhaps most importantly of all, they need to engage with case-study examples of resistance to racism and to be familiar with the letter and spirit of anti-discrimination legislation in the UK. These arguments continue to be part of the debate about citizenship education in Bradford, as indeed elsewhere.

Raising achievement

There is as yet no demonstrable causal connection between the citizenship curriculum in particular and achievement at 16+ in general. It can certainly be hypothesised, however, that such a connection exists, or will exist.

First, it is reasonable to expect that the citizenship curriculum will raise pupils' pride in their own identity and community.[7] This in turn helps pupils feel confident in their own abilities and to have high aspirations and from such confidence comes academic success.

There is tentative evidence for this argument in the data that Bradford collects on success in GCSE exams at 16+. Attainment in religious studies (RS) and religious education (RE) is consistently high when compared with other subjects. In 2002, for example, 54 per cent of students taking RS (full course GCSE) gained A*-C grades and 41 per cent of students taking RE (short course GCSE). This compares with Bradford's average for five A*-C grades at 35.6 per cent. The percentages refer to high raw figures – 1,350 students took RS in 2002 and 1,577 students took RE.[8]

There are many possible explanations for the phenomenon. But it is reasonable to speculate that students are more successful in RS and RE than in other subjects because they are able to draw on their own cultural and religious backgrounds and because teachers are informed about and empathetic towards their backgrounds.

Second, the vision of British society as a community of communities helps young people of all ethnicities to see and feel that they have a stake in it, and a valuable and valued part to play in the next phase of its evolutionary progress. It is reasonable to suppose that the self-confidence that flows from the vision will feed into the learning and study of all subjects.

Third, the citizenship curriculum has the potential to break down mutual antagonisms within a school and in this way to give all learners a greater sense of security and safety. Feeling safe, both emotionally and physically, is an essential foundation for successful learning.

A fourth way in which attainment may be raised by this initiative is through teachers' professional development as they engage with the issues in both their planning and their teaching. One of the real professional challenges of this curriculum, and indeed of citizenship as a whole, is that it requires teachers to lower their guard and to engage in the learning and exploration process with their pupils as fellow human beings. There are many times when the teachers will not know the answers because the questions are too complex. The confidence to say 'I don't know' has to exist in teachers' hearts so that pupils too can recognise that they don't need to know all the answers. No one can ever know all there is to know about cultures and religions, not least because there is so much diversity within as well between different groups. Openness to learning and willingness to ask questions are essential for teachers if they are to engage successfully with the issues raised by the citizenship curriculum.

11 DOING SOMETHING RIGHT
– ethos, leadership and policy

SUMMARY

How a school is led and managed is clearly of vital importance. This final chapter discusses the principal features of sound management and inspiring leadership, drawing on the experience of three schools in Leeds and two in Sheffield. It closes by recalling the wider social and international context within which leadership has to be exercised and by listing the themes and threads which run through this book as a whole. The chapter draws on papers by Sameena Choudry; formerly a teacher adviser in Sheffield; Judi Hall, head of Shakespeare Primary School, Leeds; Colleen Jackson, head of Quarry Mount Primary School, Leeds; and John Martin, assistant head of Allerton Grange High School, Leeds.

Vision and action

Through the 1990s the education system laid great stress on raising educational standards. By conventional measures, such as SATs scores and GCSE results, there was considerable success. There continues to be, however, a wide range of attainment across the socio-economic and between pupils of different community backgrounds. For example, as demonstrated in Chapter 3, there is a significant gap between national averages and the attainment of children and young people of Pakistani heritage. There are signs that the gap may be closing. If indeed it is closing, this is probably due in large part to greater involvement of parents and communities; to the contribution of LEA advisers, inspectors, advisory teachers and EMA teachers; and to the quality of leadership in schools – headteachers, governors, senior and middle management.

Leeds LEA identified six schools which, on the basis of comparative performance data, appeared to be especially successful in raising the achievement of British Pakistani learners, either overall or in particular subjects.[1] The headteachers and their senior colleagues were invited to consider the factors underlying their success. 'We must be doing something right,' mused one of them, though could not with confidence be sure what it was. She and colleagues in other schools did,

however, speculate and in doing so pointed the way for further reflection and research. Reflections from three of the six schools are described in this chapter. The chapter also contains reflections on the same subject from two schools in Sheffield.

One of the schools identified by LEA monitoring was Quarry Mount Primary. The school serves the tenth most deprived ward in England: just over a half the pupils are severely affected by economic disadvantage. Sixty-four per cent are of minority ethnic backgrounds and between them speak over twenty languages.

The headteacher engaged staff – and later governors, parents and pupils – in articulating a vision of education that would inform subsequent planning and lead to specific projects. There are extracts from the statement in box 42. The projects informed by the statement included:

- revising the race equality policy in accordance with the Stephen Lawrence Inquiry report and the Race Relations (Amendment) Act and sending copies to all stakeholders

- tracking by the EMA teacher of the progress of a group of pupils; they were assessed at the beginning and end of the year and the results were reported to staff, governors and parents

- developing an EMA council (along the lines of a school council), of two parents, two governors and four elected Year 6 pupils, led by the headteacher

- enabling Muslim mothers to benefit from EAL courses, through making home visits to explain the courses; providing crèche facilities and transport to and from class; and making the courses women-only.

In its first year of operation the activities of the EMA council included:

- receiving and discussing reports on the progress of targeted groups and forwarding views to the governing body

- reports by the pupil members to the pupil body at assemblies

- sending a questionnaire to all parents, staff and children on the impact of Black History Month celebrations and using the findings in the planning of future celebrations.

Structure, stimulus and support

At Allerton Grange School, Leeds, the attainment of Pakistani heritage and African Caribbean students was very poor in 2001 and 2002, both at KS3 and at 16+. The school took focused measures to improve the attainment of these two groups, as described in box 43. The results of Pakistani heritage students at KS3 in summer 2003 showed a striking, indeed spectacular, improvement. At the time of writing, it is too soon to judge with confidence whether improvements were caused directly by the focused extra provision. The project is nevertheless of considerable professional and communal interest, and has been commended by the DfES.[2] Its features include a great emphasis on building and maintaining relationships with parents and amongst the whole staff; a mix of academic and pastoral concerns; and a readiness to be entirely open and explicit about issues on which other schools may be inclined to keep a low profile.

Box 42

Vision and action
– the school as a learning community

'Vision without action is merely a dream. Action without vision is pointless. Vision and action together can change the world.'
Nelson Mandela

... We believe that, to create a socially cohesive and culturally rich society, we need to encourage in our children a strong sense of moral qualities, including honesty, trust and respect for others. We need to help them to develop an understanding of and respect for a wide range of religious values, languages and cultural traditions; as well as teaching them the rights and responsibilities they have as citizens.

... We will prepare them to play an active role as citizens and to develop a healthy, safer lifestyle. We will teach them to develop good relationships and respect the differences between people.

We will help children to develop lively, enquiring minds, the ability to question and argue rationally and apply themselves to tasks and physical skills with increasing independence...

Our school recognises, and builds upon, early experiences gained in the home and pre-school setting, and provides a secure foundation upon which later stages of education can build. Ours is a school that welcomes parents, carers and the extended family. Working in partnership, using a holistic approach to education, benefits the child, school, parent/carers and community.

Our school strives to be one where all stakeholders are on-going learners...

Source: vision statement by Quarry Mount Primary School, Leeds, 2001

Box 43

Leadership, management and first results
– a school-based special project

Background

Almost 38 per cent of the students at Allerton Grange School, Leeds are of Pakistani heritage. Analysis of performance data shows that along with African-Caribbean students they were achieving substantially poorer results than other students.

The senior management team set up the Ethnic Minority Achievement Project (EMAP), to focus on 60 pupils in Years 7, 9 and 10. Half were of Pakistani heritage, half of African-Caribbean. Half were boys, half girls. The pupils who were selected for the project were considered to be on the borderline between 4 and 5 at Key Stage 3 or on the C/D borderline at GCSE. The project would be a three-year, intensive programme of intervention and support with the very specific aim of raising achievement levels.

The project's structure

A leadership and management structure was devised that involved the integration of a range of initiatives and support teams under a common senior manager, so that a variety of funding streams and resources, both human and material, could be mobilised. It was decided in this connection to integrate EMAP with the Excellence Challenge initiative and use resources from the Gifted and Talented and Learning Support strands of Excellence in Cities (EiC). This gave the project access to the learning mentor team and to activities developed through other EiC programmes.

In its first year, the EMAP team consisted of three learning mentors and three EMA support staff, and was led by an assistant headteacher. It met weekly to share progress and good practice, and its minutes were circulated widely to other staff. An essential part of its work was student support and observation in lessons, and this raised awareness of the team's aims and concerns amongst colleagues.

Partnerships with parents

Once the target group was identified, the parents were involved. An introductory letter was followed up by a phone call to arrange a home visit. Any worries about what the project might entail were quickly dispelled once its aims were explained and parents welcomed the individual attention their child would receive. Parents were then kept up to date with progress via phone calls and a termly newsletter produced by the EMAP students themselves.

Pupil participation and involvement

Targeted students had an initial mentoring session aimed at introducing them to the project, explaining why it would be good for them and enabling the mentor to target future provision effectively. A common proforma was used to record information about academic strengths and weaknesses, and about personal likes, dislikes, interests and activities. Later mentoring sessions involved setting achievement targets and planning appropriate support programmes.

Enrichment Activities

In addition to the individual mentoring and in-class support the pupils took part in a variety of activities designed to motivate them to aim higher academically. These included the national *Aim Higher* roadshow, university activity days, college taster courses, educational visits, *Getaway Girls* sessions and research on positive role models that was written up in the newsletter.

First signs of success

After the first year of the three-year programme, the results were striking. Sixty-two per cent of Pakistani heritage pupils achieved level 5 or above: 52 percentage points better than the previous year and only five points below the average for the whole school. The proportion achieving level 5 amongst those who were involved in EMAP was 80 per cent. In maths and science at KS3 Pakistani heritage students improved on the previous year by 26 and 29 percentage points respectively. For the EMAP group the increases were 31 points in maths and 41 points in science.

Source: Allerton Grange School, Leeds

Box 44 contains quotations from students on the Allerton Grange programme. They show clearly the kinds of gain in confidence that the students experienced and the higher expectations of themselves that they formed.

Box 44

Even if you're a nobody
– some students' views

Comments from students involved in the Ethnic Minority Achievement Project (EMAP) at Allerton Grange School, Leeds

If you believe in yourself you can achieve anything even if you start off as a nobody.

If you put your mind to anything you can achieve it.

If you have a big enough dream you can succeed which can apply to other things as well.

EMAP has encouraged me by helping me do better in subjects that I find difficult.

EMAP has helped me to think about what I would like to do in the future and improved my behaviour in school.

Helping me with my problems and how to control them.

We all meet up in the City Learning Centre and discuss what has been happening in school. We ask each other questions and advise each other how to get on better. We also do revising on computers.

I had been thinking about university but not in depth. Now I know what university is really like, I want to attend. All the opportunities university has to offer are endless and a chance like this I wouldn't want to miss out on.

For me I didn't really have strong intentions on going to university. The Aim Higher Roadshow really gave me an opportunity to look into uni and consider my future there. As a result I am definitely attending. Thanks to the informative session brought to my attention by EMAP and hosted by Aim Higher.

Source: student evaluation forms, Allerton Grange High School, Leeds

---

Prizing policy

A key factor in any initiative to effect change is the formulation and implementation of policy. Negotiated and agreed policy is a vehicle for asserting values, securing commitments to courses of action and measuring and marking strategic direction. To foster the development of sound policies in schools, the Race Equality Advisory Forum (REAF) in Leeds established the annual Stephen Lawrence Education Award in 1999/2000. It was the first scheme of its kind in the country. Its purpose is to:

- acknowledge and celebrate existing good practice in promoting race equality and achievement in schools

- encourage all schools to place a commitment to race equality at the centre of curriculum, policy and practice

- provide a focus for race equality initiatives in schools throughout the city

- provide an opportunity for schools to share effective practice.

Schools that apply for the award are judged against ten criteria. These are to do with recruitment of staff, positive action, dealing with racist incidents, monitoring and target-setting by ethnicity, staff and governor training, curriculum design and development, and innovative practice. In 2003, schools which demonstrated successful practice against all ten criteria included Quarry Mount School, described earlier in this chapter, and Shakespeare Primary School. Extracts from a report by the latter are shown in box 45.

Reflections by senior management

Chapter 5 described how Sheffield LEA identified two secondary schools where the academic results of Pakistani heritage students, particularly boys, were strikingly good. As well as interviewing some of the boys about the reasons for their success, a researcher interviewed senior staff in the same schools. Box 46 gives part of the interview transcript. Six main factors emerged as contributing to the success in raising achievement and may be summarised as follows.

Addressing pastoral needs.

The schools saw themselves as strongly student-centred and caring, with teachers committed to listening and responding to what students say.

Inclusiveness

The schools prided themselves on being truly comprehensive in terms of social class as well as ethnicity. Pakistani heritage students formed the largest minority ethnic group in both schools but also there were students from several other backgrounds. Parents of minority ethnic students belonged to a range of social classes and occupational groups.

Curricular provision relevant to Pakistani heritage learners

One school had specialist language college status and in consequence linguistic skills were particularly highly valued. There was accreditation in Urdu at GCSE, AS and A2.

Readiness to experiment

One school had been experimenting with single sex classes in science. The results of this particular project had been encouraging. More significantly, in the view of senior staff, the project signalled that the school was ready to try out new possibilities.

Positive role models

The schools were keen to attract applications from minority ethnic staff who would act as role models. An added benefit was that such colleagues have insights and understandings regarding the needs of minority ethnic students and can provide invaluable assistance in communication between the school and parents.

Effective links with homes and the community

The schools are proactive in engaging with their minority ethnic communities. For example, on Friday afternoons Muslim staff are timetabled so that they can participate in the Jum'ah prayer at mosques in the area.

Two kinds of leadership

A distinction is sometimes made between 'transactional' leadership and 'transformational'. The Commission on the Future of Multi-Ethnic Britain pointed out that the distinction is particularly relevant to issues of equality and diversity:

continued on page 84

Box 45

Will never be finished
– commitments at a primary school

... We do not view our diversity as a problem but as a wonderful resource to share and provide a richness to our curriculum.

Multicultural education' is not something we do ... One-off events, occasional inclusion or special days do not create the ethos of diversity and richness that we see on a daily basis. The work is infused into everything we do and cannot be separated out from our everyday curriculum...

Awareness of this diversity underpins our school development and improvement plan and our EMA plan. An effective plan will meet the following criteria:

- It will have a clear strategic view and sense of direction

- The results of monitoring and evaluation will be used to determine priorities

- The priorities will be clearly identified

- Targets and success criteria will show evidence of improvement

- Targets will be specific and measurable

- The plan will clearly be linked to resources and finance

- Senior management, teachers and governors will have a clear oversight of the plan

- All staff and governors will be involved.

This way of planning, monitoring and evaluation is now embedded in how we work ... and all staff are familiar with the process. The achievement of pupils from minority ethnic groups is carefully planned, targeted and an integral part of what we do. The continual push to improve the range and quality of experiences that we offer our children is something which is kept high on the agenda so that staff, governors, parents and community all know that this is something we do every day...

The work on antiracism and celebrating cultural diversity will never be finished as we have a continual turnover of pupils and parents, and new links with community groups and recruit new staff, but the school development and improvement plan and the EMA plan allow us to be focused and clear about our achievements and how we can make further improvements.

Source: Shakespeare Primary School, Leeds

Box 46

Reasons for success – interviews with senior staff

SCHOOL A

What in your opinion has been the single most important factor in the overall success of Pakistani boys in your school?

I think it's to do with the whole pastoral climate of the school, which is very special... It's been built up over many years. I am told that we have a good reputation for pastoral care across the city. Students of Pakistani heritage are included in this as much as anybody else.

Do you think that there are any other factors that have contributed to your school's overall success in raising the attainment of Pakistani boys?

I would like to think that it is something as nebulous as finding the climate of the school and the general ethos of the school accepting. And it's really often quite amazing and heart warming that, given our diversity, we have very few racial problems. And if we talk to students themselves, and I do a lot of that, they say that this is a comfortable place... Strong messages come from the headteacher and the rest of the senior management team regarding the positive attitudes we adopt towards diversity. This strong message has been sent out for many years.

So you feel that this strong message is a key factor?

It's much more than a message. It is the identity of the school. We do not see ourselves or identify ourselves simply as a high-flying academic school, though we know we have that dimension to us. Nor do we see ourselves as a white middle class school. That's not what we are, not what we are about, that's not how we want to present ourselves. We genuinely present ourselves as a diverse school, a totally comprehensive school, which welcomes students of whatever ethnicity, whatever faith and home language, and then we show them that we mean what we say and we will cater for all to the best of our ability. If you go to the opening pages of our prospectus you will see it clearly written there... And of course we have governors who are part and parcel of this identity and they, along with the head and senior management team, are committed and give us a lead.

SCHOOL B

What would you say has been the main factor in the overall academic success of boys of Pakistani heritage in your school?

Role models. I think it's the number of role models. We have a large number of Muslim and Asian role models at all levels.

Has the school made a conscious decision to recruit more teachers from ethnic minority backgrounds?

I'd hate to think that we just appointed somebody for the sake of it but I don't think schools and headteachers can ignore the fact that their schools should have a staff reflective of society at large and of their particular school community.

What other factors have contributed?

I suppose home-school links. For parents of the first generation and, to a certain extent, second generation, communication is a key issue. A lot of times when you want to send a message home from school, we have the staff who can do that, who can translate the message between the teacher and parent, if needed. As a result our parents feel more comfortable in coming to school.

Also is it quite handy when you live in the catchment area. You can pop into the home to do a visit when needed. Parents see me as part of the community. We also have a science teacher who lives in the catchment area. He is a positive role model who is also a Hafiz. He helps out in the mosque when there is a shortage of teachers and this means going way beyond the role in the job description as well as the traditional relationship between a school and its community. All this sends out a message to the community.

Source: interviews conducted by Sameena Choudry, 2003

Box 47

Context and controversy – comments, outlooks and concerns

Positive identity

...There are platoons of young Muslims roaming the streets. They saw the TV images of the intifada and copied them during the Oldham riots. Now they are seeing bin Laden turned by the BBC and others into a glamorous, Rambo figure. Next time, will they be copying the bombers? We have to invest in forging a positive identity for them so we create the right kind of Muslim

Fuad Nahdi, quoted in The Guardian, 24.9.01

Oppressive

Attempts to tackle racism without also tackling Islamophobia will be futile ... Race equality legislation has reduced the Muslims, the largest minority in Britain, to a deprived and disadvantaged community, almost in a state of siege ... Much as Muslims want to confront racism, they have become disillusioned with an antiracism movement that refuses to combat Islamophobia and which, in many instances, is as oppressive as the establishment itself.

Q News, March 1999

Despicable

Christ commands it ...What a disgrace if a race so despicable, degenerate and enslaved by demons should overcome a people endowed with faith in almighty God and resplendent in the name of Christ! Let those who fought against brothers and relatives now rightfully fight against the barbarians under the guidance of the Lord.

Pope Urban II, Council of Clermont 1095, launching the Crusades

Amazingly complex notion

Call me a filthy racist – go on, you know you want to – but we have reason to be suspicious of Islam... I believe that mindless, ill-sorted Islamophilia is just as dangerous as mindless, ill-sorted Islamophobia. I know how dedicated it is to the cause of dumbing down but the BBC should try to take this amazingly complex notion on board.

Julie Burchill, The Guardian, 2001

Rationally and patiently

'Islam' and 'the West' are simply inadequate as banners to follow blindly... Demonisation of the Other is not a sufficient basis for any kind of decent politics...Those of us with a possibility for reaching people who are willing to listen – and there are many such people – must try to do so as rationally and as patiently as possible.

Edward Said, in Voices for Peace, autumn 2001

Took leave

The constabulary is terrified of being accused of institutional racism and would probably charge a brick wall with harassment if a Muslim drove into it... 'Religiously aggravated threatening behaviour' is a new crime invented in the mad, hysterical weeks after the Twin Towers outrage... During this period most politicians simply took leave of their senses...

Peter Hitchens, 'Can we no longer argue with a Muslim?' Mail on Sunday, 27 October 2002

Breakdown of the imagination

Whatever its immediate apparent outcome, the war on Iraq represents a catastrophic breakdown of the British and American imagination. We've utterly failed to comprehend the character of the people whose lands we have invaded, and for that we're likely to find ourselves paying a price beside which the body-count on both sides in the Iraqi conflict will seem trifling.

Jonathan Raban, The Guardian, 19 April 2003

Restoring peace

While they smash our pubs we must boycott their shops. It's the only way to make the Asian community bring their young thugs under control, and restore peace to Oldham.

Nick Griffin and the BNP, or the pro-Muslim Labour Party?

Election leaflets in Oldham, 2001

A different America

My detestation [of Bush and Rumsfeld] ... has nothing to do with anti-Americanism. Quite the reverse. I resent the posturing and the policy because I know a different America – a United States which is the land of the lucid and literate, as well as the free and the brave – a country with citizens, from sea to shining sea, who believe in peace and justice.

Roy Hattersley, The Guardian, 31 March 2003

There must be efficient management ('transactional leadership') concerned with the setting of goals and objectives, and holding staff accountable for achieving them. Such management can be summarised in terms of abilities that can be imparted through training courses and assessed with reasonable accuracy.

'Transformational leadership' is concerned with personal qualities rather than abilities. These include empathy, openness to criticism, a degree of judicious risk-taking, enthusiasm, an aptitude for articulating a vision of how the organisation could be different and better, and a readiness to challenge and shape the opinions of others rather than pander to them.[3]

In a context of overload and uncertainty, of competing proposals, demands and expectations, and of vast geopolitical anxiety, transformational leadership keeps its head and its heart. The nine quotations in box 47 were used in a values clarification activity during a leadership training experience in 2003. The juxtaposition of conflicting and competing views in such an activity is a vivid reminder of the wider social, political and international context in which leadership has to be exercised.[4]

One of the tasks of a transformational leader is to encourage and enable colleagues to wrestle with issues of moment and meaning – not by providing answers but by enabling them to cope with controversy and complexity; not by a finished product but by a focused process. It is perhaps the most challenging and potentially most rewarding of all the tasks of transformational leadership, and arguably the one most in need of development. This is work in progress, work in process.

In the end, what's worth fighting for?

Transformational leadership involves knowing, amongst other things, what's worth fighting for.[5] This book draws now to an end with a list (see box 48) of its principal themes and threads. The list is derived from discussions and reflections amongst those who took part in the RAISE project in 2002-04 and summarises succinctly what, finally, is worth fighting for.

Box 48

Themes and Threads
– what's worth fighting for

Empathy
Empathy with young British Pakistani people, the pressures on them from a range of different directions, their determination, their spirit; empathy with their parents and communities

Listening
Listening to British Pakistani children and young people, and being alert to their wishes, aspirations and anxieties, and to how they and their communities are changing

Fairness
Holding the line and the balance between competing demands and pressures; taking a principled stand on the importance of fair play and process

Procedural neutrality
Ensuring that different points of view get a fair hearing, but also that all are questioned, reviewed and discussed

Teachers as researchers
Teachers need time and space to reflect on their own practice, as individuals, teams and whole staffs, and to devise their own ways of improving it

Critical understanding
Critical understanding of religion and religions, and of religion as part both of the problem and of the solution

Muddling through
Accepting that the best can be the enemy of the good, that there is seldom enough knowledge or evidence before action has to be taken, that uncertainty is frequently the name of the game, or much of the game

The culture of the school
Giving focused thought and attention to how your whole school, and also individual parts of it, can embody in daily routine and culture the qualities and values listed above

Hope
Carrying on, despite setbacks and opposition, self-critically but with resolution and determination.

Source: the RAISE project, 2002-04

CHAPTER NOTES

Chapter 1

1   The conversation is derived and adapted from focus group discussion at a school in Rotherham, summer 2003. Amongst English-heritage people the word Paki is almost invariably derogatory. There is a trend amongst young Pakistani heritage people themselves, however, to reclaim the word as a badge of pride. Pak means pure and Pakistan is the land of the pure.

2   In 1947 the country known as India was split into two, India and Pakistan. The latter had two parts, West Pakistan and East Pakistan, several hundred miles apart from each other. All its citizens were known as Pakistanis. Subsequently West Pakistan and East Pakistan became two separate countries, Pakistan and Bangladesh. This book is about British people whose background is in the country now known as Pakistan and previously as West Pakistan.

3   See *Islamic Britain: religion, politics and identity among British Muslims* by Philip Lewis, I B Tauris 1994.

4   For fuller discussion see *Islamophobia: issues, challenges and action* by the Commission on British Muslims and Islamophobia, Trentham Books 2004.

Chapter 2

1   Merryl Wynn Davies, *New Internationalist*, May 2002.

2   *Q News*, quoted in the 1997 report of the Commission on British Muslims and Islamophobia, p 17.

3   Faisal Bodi, *Q News*, February 2000, quoted in Lewis (2002)

    The latter paper is also available on the internet and is extremely pertinent to the themes of this chapter, and indeed of this whole book. It can be found at the website of the Bradford Race Review, www.bradford2020.com/pride.

4   Yunas Samad (1998), quoted in Lewis (see above).

Chapter 3

1   DfES, *Statistics of Education: pupil progress by characteristics*, 2002. See also Bhattacharyya *et al* (2003).

2   The report of the Commission on the Future of Multi Ethnic Britain (200) p377.

Chapter 4

1   For fuller information see *Views, Voices and Visibility: realising the achievement of Muslim pupils of Pakistani and Kashmiri heritage* by Nicola Davies at www.insted.co.uk.

2   See for example Gillborn and Youdell (2000).

3   There is fuller information about the course at http://www.eslmainstream.com.

Chapter 5

1   The figures are given for background purposes only and need to be treated with some caution and within the context of small numbers of pupils of Pakistani heritage within the Year 11 cohort overall for the LEA (273 Pakistani heritage for the LEA altogether compared to 5744 in the Year 11 cohort in the LEA as a whole). The number of students of Pakistani heritage in the Year 11 cohort for each

school is quite small, 12 in school A and 19 in school B. In both schools the proportion of students with minority ethnic backgrounds is around 25 per cent and in both the largest single group is of Pakistani or Kashmiri heritage.

2   But in the paper on which this chapter is based, *Factors contributing to the educational success of boys of Pakistani heritage in two secondary schools in Sheffield* by Sameena Choudry, the schools are described separately. The full article, together with the questionnaires and interview schedules which Sameena Choudry used, can be read at www.insted.co.uk/raise.

3   In this excerpt from the researcher's transcripts, as in all other extracts in this chapter, the students' names have been changed.

Chapter 7

1   Maurice Coles, *Education and Islam: a new strategic approach*, published by the School Development Support Agency, Room 114, Town Hall, Leicester LE1 9BG.

2   There is fuller information at www.supplementary schools.org.uk.

3   BASS, Martineau Centre, Balden Road, Harborne, Birmingham B32 2EH.

4   The website is at www.bgfl.org/supplementary.

5   The research reports are published by the School of Education, 21 University Road, University of Leicester, Leicester LE1 7RF

Chapter 8

1   The names of the schools have been changed, as have those of students and parents quoted later in the chapter.

2   There is reference to the meetings and discussions with Year 6 pupils at the beginning of chapter 2.

3   None of the events described here took place in Rotherham. The stories were created in this form by the Insted consultancy for staff training sessions in various parts of the country.

4. The research in Manchester is described in a paper by Musarat Malik that can be read at www.insted.co.uk/raise

Chapter 9

1   The distinction was famously developed by Jim Cummins at the University of Toronto. There is discussion at www.iteachilearn.com/cummins/bicscalp.html and explanations in McWilliam (1998) and Brent Language Service (2000). See also Leung (2002) and Conteh (2003).

2   Fiona Lingard and Tania Sanders. There is fuller information at www.insted.co.uk/raise. For a substantial academic evaluation of Bradford's *Talking Partners* programme see Kotler *et al* (2001).

3   The test was originally developed in the 1960s by Catherine Renfrew in her work as a speech and language therapist.

4   Inverted commas for the word 'behind' since the concept of test age is simply a theoretical construct for identifying

children below the median level. Contrary to common sense, it was not related to notions to how long time it might take for a child to 'catch up'. When the test was standardised (on English mother tongue speakers, incidentally) 50 per cent of all children had a test age, by definition, which was above their chronological or real age and 50 per cent had a test age which was below.

5 *Writing in English as an Additional Language at KS4 and post-16,* 74 pages including appendices, available from Ofsted free of charge.

Chapter 10

1 *Community Pride not Prejudice,* the report of a committee chaired by Sir Herman (later Lord) Ouseley. The later reports in 2001 were by Cantle, Clark, Home Office and Ritchie. For a fuller discussion see chapter 9 of Commission on British Muslims and Islamophobia (2004).

2 Miller (2004) at www.insted.co.uk/raise. There is fuller information about developments in Bradford at www.ngfl.ac.uk . (Go to 'Schemes of Work', then to (Bradford's Enhanced Citizenship Curriculum'.)

3 Connolly (2000).

4 Short and Carrington (1995)

5 For a broad outline of the stories of British Pakistani people in Bradford, see chapter I.

6 For extensive discussion, see the opening chapters of the report of the Commission on the Future of Multi-Ethnic Britain (2000).

7 It is relevant to recall that the high-achieving students quoted in chapter 5 attributed their success, in part, to the fact that they felt their schools recognised and affirmed their personal, religious and cultural identity.

8 These statistics do not include private schools in Bradford.

9 Commission on the Future of Multi-Ethnic Britain (2000).

Chapter 11

1 The six schools were Allerton Grange High School, City of Leeds School, Quarry Mount Primary, Primrose Hill High School, Roundhay School and Shakespeare Primary.

2 *Aiming High: raising the achievement of minority ethnic pupils,* DfES 2003, pp 21-22.

3 Commission on the Future of Multi-Ethnic Britain (2000), p 281, drawing on work by Beverley Alimo-Metcalfe.

4 The issues raised in box 47 are discussed at length in the 2004 report of the Commission on British Muslims and Islamophobia. See in particular chapters 2-4. There are also valuable discussions in Ahmed (2003), Jacobson (2003), Muslim Council of Britain (2002), Ramadan (2003) and Shain (2003).

5 The phrase is taken from Fullan and Hargreaves (1996).

Case Studies

This book has been informed by case studies written in the following LEAs.

Bradford
Case study by Joyce Miller about Bradford's enhanced citizenship curriculum

Derby
Case study by Tania Sanders about the *Talking Partners* programme originally developed in Bradford

Kirklees
Case studies by Monica Deb about classroom action research and about school-parent contacts by Shazia Azhar and Jo Pilling

Leeds
Case studies about whole-school policies and school-based special projects by Davinder Bains, Jean Clennell, Judi Hall, Gary Lovelace, Colleen Jackson, John Martin and Liz Wren

Leicester
Case study by Maurice Irfan Coles about contacts between mainstream schools and madrasahs

Manchester
Case study by Musarat Malik about girls' progress and achievements

Nottingham
Case study by Stuart Scott about the involvement of parents in their children's education

Redbridge
Case studies by Jannis Abley, Bill Gent and Samina Jaffar about contacts with parents, imams and mosques

Rotherham
Case study by Mary Sculthorpe about the creation of a new secondary school

Sheffield
Case study by Sameena Choudry about the views of students and senior staff at two secondary schools

Slough
Case study by Nicola Davies about the reasons for under-achievement.

Please note: most of the case studies can be read at www.insted.co.uk/raise.

BIBLIOGRAPHY

(All publishers are in London, except where indicated)

Ahmed, Akbar (2003) *Islam under Siege: living dangerously in a post-honor world,* Cambridge: Polity Press

Ahmed, Nafeez and Faisal Bodi, Raza Kazim and Massoud Shadjareh (2001) *The Oldham Riots: discrimination, deprivation and communal tension in the United Kingdom,* Islamic Human Rights Commission

Allen, Christopher (2003) *Fair Justice: the Bradford disturbances, the sentencing and the impact,* Forum Against Islamophobia and Racism

Allen, Christopher and Jørgen Nielsen (2002) *Summary Report on Islamophobia in the European Union after 11 September 2001,* Vienna: European Monitoring Centre on Racism and Xenophobia

Ali, Monica (2003) *Brick Lane,* Doubleday

Anwar, Mohammed and Qadir Bakhsh (2003) *British Muslims and State Policies,* Warwick: Centre for Research in Ethnic Relations

Bell, David (2003) *Access and Achievement in Urban Education: ten years on,* Fabian Society

Bhattacharyya, Gargi, Lisa Ison and Maud Blair (2003) *Minority Ethnic Achievement and Progress in Education and Training: the evidence,* Department for Education and Skills

Birt, Yahya (2001) *Being a Real Man in Islam: drugs, criminality and the problem of masculinity,* http://homepage.ntlworld.com/masud/ISLAM/misc/drugs.htm

Brent Language Service (2000) *Enriching Literacy: talk, text and tales in today's classroom,* Stoke on Trent: Trentham Books

Bunglawala, Inayat (2002) It's Getting Harder To Be A British Muslim, *The Observer,* 19 May

Cantle, Ted chair (2001) *Community Cohesion: a report of the independent review team,* Home Office

Clark, Tony (2001) *Burnley Speaks, Who Listens?* Burnley MBC

Coles, Maurice Irfan (2004) *Education and Islam: a new strategic approach,* Leicester: School Development Support Agency

Commission on British Muslims and Islamophobia (2004), *Islamophobia: issues, challenges and action,* Stoke on Trent: Trentham Books

Commission on British Muslims and Islamophobia (1997), *Islamophobia, a challenge for us all,* Runnymede Trust

Commission on the Future of Multi-Ethnic Britain (2000) *The Future of Multi-Ethnic Britain: the Parekh Report,* Profile Books

Connolly, Paul (2000) What Now for the Contact Hypothesis? – towards a new research agenda, *Race Ethnicity and Education,* vol.3 no.2, June

Conteh, Jean (2003) *Succeeding in Diversity. Culture, language and learning in Primary Classrooms,* Stoke on Trent: Trentham

Davies, Merryl Wyn (2002) Wilful Imaginings, *New Internationalist,* no. 345, May

Department for Education and Skills (2003) *Aiming High: raising the achievement of minority ethnic pupils*

Fullan, Michael and Andy Hargreaves (1996) *What's Worth Fighting for in your School,* New York: Teachers College Press

Gillborn, David and Deborah Youdell (2000) *Rationing Education: policy, reform and equity,* Buckingham: Open University Press

Haddock, Maureen (2003) *Community Cohesion Initiatives in Oldham Primary Schools,* Oldham Metropolitan Borough Council

Imran, Muhammad and Elaine Miskell (2003) *Citizenship and Muslim Perspectives: teachers sharing ideas,* Birmingham: Development Education Centre

Jacobson, Jessica (2003) *Islam in Transition: Religion and Identity Among British Pakistani Youth,* Routledge

Kirklees Metropolitan Council (2003) *Safe Children Sound Learning: Guidance for Madressahs,* Kirklees MBC

Kotler, Angie, Martin Levoi and Rupert Wegerif (2001) Oracy and the educational achievement of pupils with English as an additional language: the impact of bringing 'Talking Partners' into Bradford schools, *Journal of Bilingual Education and Bilingualism,* vol 4, no 6

Kundnani, Arun (2001) *From Oldham to Bradford: the violence of the violated,* Institute of Race Relations

Kundnani, Arun (2002) *An Unholy Alliance? – racism, religion and communalism,* Institute of Race Relations, 30 July

Lewis, Philip (2002) Between Lord Ahmed and Ali G: which future for British Muslims?, in W.A.R. Shahid and P.S. van Koningsfeld, eds, *Religious Freedom and the Neutrality of the State: the position of Islam in the European Union,* Leuven: Peeters

Leung, Constant ed (2002) *Language and additional language issues in school education: a reader for teachers,* NALDIC

Luton Borough Council (2003) *Sticking Together, Embracing Diversity: report of the community cohesion scrutiny panel*, Luton

McWilliam, Norah (1998) *What's in a Word? – vocabulary development in multilingual classrooms*, Stoke on Trent: Trentham Books

Mehmood, Tariq (2003) *While there is Light*, Comma Press

Modood, Tariq (2003) Muslims and the Politics of Difference, in Sarah Spencer, (ed) *The Politics of Migration*, Oxford: Blackwell and *Political Quarterly* 74 (1), pp.100-115

Muslim Council of Britain (2002) *The Quest for Sanity: reflections on September 11 and the aftermath*, Muslim Council of Britain

Muslim Liaison Committee (2001) *Revised Guidelines on Meeting the Religious and Cultural Needs of Muslim Pupils*, Birmingham Central Mosque

National Association of Schoolmasters and Union of Women Teachers (2003) *Islamophobia: advice for schools and colleges*, NASUWT

Ofsted (2003) *Boys' Achievement in Secondary Schools*, Ofsted

Ouseley, Herman (2001) *Community Pride Not Prejudice: making diversity work in Bradford*, Bradford: Bradford Vision

Ramadan, Tariq (2003) *Western Muslims and the Future of Islam,* Oxford University Press

Ramadan, Tariq (1999) *To be a European Muslim: a study of Islamic sources in the European context*, Leicester: The Islamic Foundation

Richardson, Robin and Berenice Miles (2003) *Equality Stories: recognition, respect and raising achievement,* Stoke on Trent: Trentham

Richardson, Robin and Angela Wood (1999) *Inclusive Schools, Inclusive Society: race and identity on the agenda*, Stoke on Trent: Trentham Books

Ritchie, David chair (2001) *Oldham Independent Review*, Oldham Metropolitan Council

Runnymede Trust (2003) *Complementing Teachers: a practical guide to promoting race equality in schools*, Granada Learning

Runnymede Trust (1993) *Equality Assurance in Schools: quality, identity, society*, Stoke on Trent: Trentham Books

Sacks, Jonathan (2002) *The Dignity of Difference: how to avoid the clash of civilisations*, Continuum

Sardar, Ziauddin and Merryl Wyn Davies (2002) *Why Do People Hate America?* Cambridge: Icon Books

Seddon, Mohammad Siddique, Dilwar Hussain and Nadeem Malik (2003) *British Muslims: loyalty and belonging,* Leicester: Islamic Foundation

Sewell, Tony (2000) *Black Masculinities and schooling – how black boys survive modern schooling*, Stoke on Trent: Trentham Books

Shain, Farzana (2003) *The Schooling and Identity of Asian Girls,* Stoke on Trent: Trentham Books

Ward, Gordon (2000) Key Strategies for a Language Enhancing Curriculum, downloadable from http://homepage.ntlworld.com/gordon.ward2000/

Ward, Gordon (2000) Including Everyone in the Literacy Hour, downloadable from http://homepage.ntlworld.com/gordon.ward2000/

White, Amanda (2002) *Social Focus in Brief: ethnicity,* Office of National Statistics

Younge, Gary (2003) The Wrong Way Round, *The Guardian*, 8 September